Guide on

Consultation and Collaboration with Indian Tribal Governments And the Public Participation of Indigenous Groups and Tribal Members in Environmental decision making

Canyon de Chelly

PREPARED BY THE

National Environmental Justice Advisory Council
Indigenous Peoples Subcommittee

A Federal Advisory Committee to the U.S. Environmental Protection Agency

NATIONAL
ENVIRONMENTAL JUSTICE
ADVISORY COUNCIL

November 22, 2000

Ms. Carol Browner, Administrator
U.S. Environmental Protection Agency
401 M Street, SW
Washington, DC 20460

RE: Guide on Tribal Consultation and Public Participation

Dear Administrator Browner:

The Indigenous Peoples Subcommittee, of the National Environmental Justice Advisory Council (NEJAC), created the enclosed "Guide on Consultation and Collaboration with Indian Tribal Governments and the Public Participation of Indigenous Groups and Tribal Members in Environmental Decision Making" to address concerns raised about the lack of effective consultation and collaboration between federal agencies and American Indian and Alaska Native tribal governments. The NEJAC hopes this Guide will help EPA, and other interested stakeholders, better understand the necessity and principles for effective consultation with tribal governments and the meaningful involvement of tribal communities and tribal members in public participation processes.

The NEJAC looks forward to the Agency's consideration of this Guide and the facilitation of any discussions and actions to bring these recommendations to fruition. If I can be of further assistance in this matter, please do not hesitate to contact me at (205) 733-0178.

Sincerely,

/signed/

Haywood Turrentine, Chairman
National Environmental Justice
Advisory Council

A Federal Advisory Committee to the U.S. Environmental Protection Agency

Disclaimer

Indigenous Peoples Subcommittee (IPS) Members:

Tom Goldtooth, Chair, Indigenous Environmental Network
Dwayne Beavers, Cherokee Nation*
Brad Hamilton, State of Kansas
Jennifer Hill-Kelly, Oneida Nation of Wisconsin
Nancy Howard, Newport News Waterworks*
George Godfrey, Haskell Indian Nations University*
Sarah James, Council of Athabascan Tribal Governments
Charles Miller, Charles Miller Law Offices
Gerald R. Prout, FMC Corporation*
Moses Squeochs, Confederated Tribes and Bands of Yakima Nation
Dean B. Suagee, Vermont Law School
Jana L. Walker, Law Office of Jana Walker**

Designated Federal Officials:

Daniel Gogal, Designated Federal Official (DFO), Office of Environmental Justice, EPA
Anthony Hanson, Alternate DFO, American Indian Environmental Office, EPA*
Bob Smith, Alternate DFO, American Indian Environmental Office, EPA**

*   Service ended in 1999
**   Service began in 2000

Acknowledgment: The IPS is thankful for the assistance of three students in the Vermont Law School Indian Country Environmental Justice Clinic in the preparation of this document: Meredith Hatfield, J.D. 1999; Kenneth Dobson, J.D. 2000; and Ivy Anderson, J.D. 2000.

**NATIONAL ENVIRONMENTAL JUSTICE ADVISORY COUNCIL
A FEDERAL ADVISORY COUNCIL TO THE
UNITED STATES ENVIRONMENTAL PROTECTION AGENCY**

November 15, 2000

The Indigenous Peoples Subcommittee, a subcommittee of the National Environmental Justice Advisory Council (NEJAC), created this "Guide on Consultation and Collaboration with Indian Tribal Governments and the Public Participation of Indigenous Groups and Tribal Members in Environmental Decision Making" to address concerns raised about the lack of effective consultation and collaboration between federal agencies and American Indian and Alaska Native tribal governments. The Guide also responds to testimony before NEJAC that, in some instances, existing public participation processes have provided inadequate opportunities for tribal communities and tribal members to have meaningful involvement in environmental and public health decision-making processes. Accordingly, the NEJAC hopes this Guide will help its readers better understand the necessity and principles for effective consultation with tribal governments and the meaningful involvement of tribal communities and tribal members in public participation processes.

Because the relationships between tribal, federal, state, and local governments continue to evolve, the NEJAC intends that the Guide be a living, dynamic document. The Indigenous Peoples Subcommittee plans to monitor this evolution and revise the Guide in consultation with the EPA's Office of Environmental Justice, American Indian Environmental Office, Tribal Operations Committee (TOC) and, as recommended by the TOC, the National Congress of American Indians. On this point, readers should note that, after the finalization of the Guide on October 17, 2000, President Clinton issued Executive Order 13175 of November 6, 2000, "Consultation and Coordination with Indian Tribal Governments." 65 Fed. Reg. 67249 (Nov. 9, 2000). The new Order strengthens the policy on tribal consultation expressed in Executive Order 13084 of May 14, 1998, which is discussed in the Guide. For the convenience of readers, a copy of the new Order is attached at the end of the Guide. The NEJAC believes that the Guide may be particularly useful to federal agencies as they take steps to comply with the new Executive Order.

Thank you for your efforts to ensure that effective consultation, collaboration, and public participation occurs within Indian country and Alaska Native villages. Please send comments or other information you wish to share with the Subcommittee to: *Designated Federal Official for the Indigenous Peoples Subcommittee, Office of Environmental Justice (2201-A), 1200 Pennsylvania Avenue, NW, Washington, DC 20460.*

Sincerely,

/signed/
Haywood Turrentine

/signed/
Tom Goldtooth

Haywood Turrentine, Chair
National Environmental Justice Advisory Council

Tom Goldtooth, Chair
Indigenous Peoples Subcommittee

INTRODUCTION

The Indigenous Peoples Subcommittee is one of six subcommittees of the National Environmental Justice Advisory Council (NEJAC), a federal advisory committee of the U.S. Environmental Protection Agency (EPA). The NEJAC believes the federal government has a responsibility to consult and collaborate with American Indian and Alaska Native tribal governments as an essential element of its trust responsibility to federally recognized tribal governments. However, the NEJAC contends that effective consultation and collaboration between federal agencies and federally recognized tribal governments is lacking. The NEJAC also believes that some existing public participation processes provide inadequate opportunities for tribal members and tribal communities to have meaningful involvement in the environmental and public health decisions affecting them.

To facilitate more effective consultation, promote genuine collaboration, and improve public participation, the Indigenous Peoples Subcommittee prepared this "Guide on Consultation and Collaboration with Indian Tribal Governments and the Public Participation of Indigenous Groups and Tribal Members in Environmental Decision Making." EPA's Office of Environmental Justice provided assistance in the development of this Guide. The Subcommittee solicited, received and applied a variety of comments on several working drafts of the Guide from tribal governments and organizations, federal agencies including various EPA offices, and other interested parties, and welcomes additional input. Accordingly, one purpose of this Guide is to inform federal agencies, as well as state and local agencies, why consultation with Indian tribal governments is an important aspect of the federal trust responsibility.

The Guide describes the sovereignty of federally recognized tribal governments and explains how they should be treated in a government-to-government fashion by federal and state agencies. It also highlights various laws and policies that require and support recognition of tribal governments as sovereign entities, and addresses the environmental and public health impacts that may adversely affect the lives of American Indian and Alaska Natives.

The Guide defines the difference between the public participation process, which is an information gathering and sharing exercise, and consultation, which is a government-to-government process that requires greater involvement and decision-making by all parties. It illustrates how both of these processes are important pathways to achieving environmental justice for tribes.

The NEJAC intends that the Guide be used as a general resource for all people and governmental agencies — whether federal, tribal, state, or local — needing information to promote environmental justice in Indian country and among Alaska Natives. Other indigenous groups may also benefit from this Guide. They include Native Hawaiian organizations, state recognized and non-recognized tribes, and community-based indigenous organizations, as well as state and local governments and businesses operating on or near Indian reservations. The NEJAC hopes that the Guide will not be considered the "final word" on tribal consultation, but instead will stimulate fresh dialogue among federal and tribal governments, as well as other interested parties. Towards that end, the NEJAC encourages the use and sharing of this Guide with all interested parties.

TABLE OF CONTENTS

EXECUTIVE SUMMARY

American Indian and Alaska Native tribes are sovereign governments recognized as self-governing under federal law. American Indians and Alaska Natives are also citizens of the United States. Because of their unique sovereign status within the federal governmental capacity of the United States, federally recognized tribes have the power to make and enforce laws on their lands, and to create governmental entities, such as tribal courts. Under its well recognized "trust responsibility" to Indian tribes, the federal government has special fiduciary obligations to protect tribal resources and uphold the rights of indigenous peoples to govern themselves on tribal lands. Many federal laws have delegated authority to tribes in recognition of their sovereign status.

The unique legal status of American Indian and Alaska Native tribes creates an important requirement for governmental entities, and other stakeholders, to understand that the federal government must consult directly with tribal governments when contemplating actions that may affect tribal lands, resources, members, and welfare. Tribal sovereignty is thwarted when federal government agencies and departments attempt to treat tribes in the same manner as any other interested members of the public, in a conventional public participation process. Rather, in recognition of their status as sovereign nations, the federal government should collaborate directly with tribal governments in a consultative process, which leads to decision-making.

Conventional *public participation* initiatives allow federal officials a means to inform affected parties about proposed future actions. As citizens of the United States, individual tribal members and tribal non-governmental organizations must be afforded the same opportunities to participate in the federal decision-making processes as would any other citizen or non-governmental organization. Though their input may be solicited, the process does not require the federal government to change its decision based on localized, public input.

On the other hand, consultation between the federal and tribal governments should be a collaborative process between government peers that seeks to reach a consensus on how to proceed. Many federal statutes specifically recognize the obligation of the federal government to consult with tribal officials on a government-to-government basis. Moreover, in some instances, specific requirements demand the federal government give special deference to tribal preferences. For example, under an order issued by Secretary of Interior Babbitt, June 4, 1997, the federal government's implementation of the Endangered Species Act (ESA) gives explicit recognition to tribal priorities.[1] This order can be considered a prototype for specifying how government-to-government consultation is to be conducted.

Similarly, other federal statutes and their implementing regulations (e.g. National Environmental Policy Act, Native American Graves Protection and Repatriation Act, National Historic Preservation Act, and American Indian Religious Freedom Act) lay the basis for recognizing tribal sovereignty through a consultation process. In each case, certain basic guiding principles should be followed: (1) tribal governments should be involved in the actual decision making process at the earliest practicable moment; (2) each agency should institutionalize its own consultation procedures for Indian governments; (3) federal agencies should train their staff on how to consult with Indian governments; and (4) integrity and honesty should always be paramount in any consultation process.

The optimal goal of tribal consultation should be to achieve consensus between tribal leaders and federal officials on how to identify, consider, and address issues or concerns. These meetings should be supplemented with broader public meetings to keep all tribal members informed. Similarly, as tribal governments create or implement their own environmental programs, public participation processes should be considered to keep all interested stakeholders (both tribal and non-tribal) in Indian country informed and to provide opportunities for meaningful involvement.

CHAPTER 1: WHY CONSULTATION WITH TRIBES IS IMPORTANT

This Chapter briefly discusses why meaningful consultation with federally recognized tribes is important. In many situations, consultation with tribes is required by law. Some of these legal authorities are discussed in Addendum A. In other situations, consultation may not be mandated by law, but should be done out of respect for the status that Indian tribes occupy in our federal system of government, as well as the unique tribal interests potentially affected.

A. The Legal Status and Rights of Tribes

Indian tribes have a special status in American law as sovereign governments. Tribes also possess certain kinds of rights that are different from the rights of other Americans. Some of the special rights of tribes are based on treaties, some are based on acts of Congress, some are based on actions taken by the Executive Branch of the Federal Government, and others are clarified by federal court rulings. Consultation with tribes must be informed by awareness of the special status and rights that tribes possess.

1. *Tribal Sovereignty*

As early as the 1830s, the U.S. Supreme Court recognized that Indian tribes are "distinct nations, independent of each other and of the rest of the world, having institutions of their own, and governing themselves by their own laws."[2] Consequently, federal law recognizes that Indian tribes possess inherent *sovereignty* over their members and their territory. Sovereignty means that tribes have the power to exercise self-determination, to make and enforce laws, and to establish courts and other forums for the resolution of disputes. The sovereignty that Indian tribes possess is *inherent*, which means that it comes from within the tribe itself and existed before the founding of the United States. It is this sovereignty that separates Indian tribes from other ethnic groups.

Under federal law, tribal sovereignty is not absolute, but rather is subject to certain limits placed on the tribes by Congress and the federal courts. According to rulings of the Supreme Court, tribes are said to retain all those aspects of their original sovereignty except aspects that have been given up in a treaty, taken away by an act of Congress, or divested by implication as a result of their dependent status.[3] Many legal scholars have criticized the Supreme Court's recent Indian law jurisprudence, particularly the implicit divestiture rule.[4] Some tribal nations do not accept certain principles of federal Indian law, such as the notion that tribes are dependent upon the federal government. In addition to inherent sovereignty, tribal governments may also exercise authority *delegated* to them by Congress.

Because tribes are governments, the relationship between tribes and the federal government is sometimes described as "government-to-government," and the President has directed each federal agency to operate within this relationship.[5] Among other things, this means that federal agencies are not to treat Indian tribes as "interest groups" or simply as part of the general public. The relationship between tribes and states can also be described as "government-to-government."

2. *The Federal Trust Responsibility*

The cornerstone of the government-to-government relationship is the federal government's *trust responsibility* to Indian tribes. Under the trust doctrine, the federal government has "charged itself with moral obligations of the highest responsibility and trust"[6] that require agencies to ensure the protection of tribal interests as they fulfill their overall missions. This doctrine has its roots in the treaties through which the tribes ceded vast portions of their aboriginal lands to the United States in exchange for the federal government's solemn promise to protect the rights of the tribes to continue to exist as self-governing nations within the lands that they reserved for themselves. The trust doctrine is also based on the practice of the federal government holding legal title to most Indian land in trust for the beneficial use of Indian tribes and tribal members. Whether or not the federal government holds legal title to Indian lands within the reservation of a particular tribe, federal law prohibits the transfer of property interests in Indian land except as authorized by Congress.

In practice, the trust responsibility gives rise to distinctive fiduciary obligations on the part of federal agencies which must be "exercised according to the strictest fiduciary standards."[7] As the Supreme Court explained, federal officials are "bound by every moral and equitable consideration to discharge the federal government's trust with good faith and fairness" when dealing with Indian tribes.[8] The trust doctrine includes duties to manage natural resources for the benefit of tribes and individual Indian landowners, and the federal government has in some cases been held liable for damage caused by mismanagement.[9]

The trust obligations are not limited solely to the management of land and other trust resources. For example, an overall "protectorate" role is reflected in Congress' express recognition that "the United States has a trust responsibility to each tribal government that includes the protection of the sovereignty of each tribal government."[10] In the modern era of tribal self-determination, tensions sometimes arise between the obligation of the federal government for the management of trust natural resources and the obligation to protect and support tribal sovereignty.

In some of the modern cases, courts have drawn a distinction between a "general trust responsibility" and a "specific trust responsibility." Specific trust responsibilities arise out of treaties, executive orders and statutes that specifically address Indian tribes and their relationships with the federal government.[11] Statutes that give agencies "comprehensive" control over the management of tribal resources also create specific trust duties. If, however, an interaction between a tribe and an agency does not involve any particular statute, regulation, or treaty specifically addressing the tribe or its resources, then the trust responsibility can be described as "general" in nature. Whether characterized as general or specific, the trust obligation imposes an additional duty with which agencies must comply when exercising discretion in carrying out their statutory duties. The general trust responsibility is not necessarily satisfied by compliance with general statutes and may impose a higher duty of protection than statutes may otherwise require.[12]

While the Bureau of Indian Affairs is the agency with the lead role in carrying out the trust responsibility, the courts have ruled that other federal agencies also have trust obligations to Indian tribes. The EPA Policy for the Administration of Environmental Programs on Indian Reservations, discussed further in Section C of this Chapter, expressly acknowledges that the trust responsibility applies to EPA.

The *plenary power* of Congress is another key doctrine of federal Indian law that is related to the trust doctrine. Under the plenary power doctrine, the federal government is vested by the Constitution with exclusive authority over relations with Indian tribes.[13] Because the power of Congress is exclusive, states generally lack governmental authority over Indian tribes and tribal members within Indian country, unless Congress has expressly delegated authority to states. The plenary power is a double-edged sword. It has been used to unilaterally take away aspects of tribal sovereignty and to exercise federal control over tribal lands and resources. On the other hand, Congress has sometimes used its plenary power to prevent state governments from interfering with tribal self-government.[14] The Supreme Court has ruled that any exercise of this power must be rationally related to the fulfillment of Congress' unique obligation toward Indian tribes.[15]

3.   *Treaty Rights*

"A treaty, including one between the United States and an Indian tribe, is essentially a contract between two sovereign nations."[16] The United States has entered into more than 400 treaties with Indian tribes. The United States is also the successor-in-interest to some treaties between tribes and the sovereigns of Europe. In the treaties, tribes typically gave up large parts of their aboriginal territories in exchange for promises from the federal government, including the promise of protection in the land they reserved to themselves. Because the United States received rights to land from the tribes, the Supreme Court has described a treaty as a grant of rights from the Indians with a reservation of those rights not granted.[17] Thus a treaty does not have to reserve expressly hunting and fishing rights within an Indian reservation for such rights to exist; rather, such on-reservation rights exist unless expressly given up.[18] In many treaties, tribes expressly reserved certain kinds of rights in lands and waters outside their reservations, such as the right to fish at usual and accustomed places.

In 1871, Congress ended the practice of entering into treaties with Indian tribes, but subsequently engaged in the practice of ratifying agreements with tribes negotiated by the Executive Branch. In addition, after treaty making ended, many reservations were established by Executive Orders. The Supreme Court has ruled that Congress has the power to break treaties with tribes, just as it has the power to break treaties with foreign countries, but unless an act of Congress shows a clear intent to break a treaty, it continues in effect.[19] Even where Congress does break a treaty, the parts of the treaty that are not broken continue in effect.

In the early years of the Republic, some tribes in the eastern United States entered into treaties with state governments. Following the passage of the 1790 Nonintercourse Act, however, such treaties are generally not legally binding because Congress did not authorize them, and are therefore void under federal law.[20]

4.   *Government-to-Government Relations*

Because Indian tribes are sovereign governments, the federal agencies are expected to carry out their dealings with the tribes in the framework of a government-to-government relationship. Basically, this means that federal officials should be aware that each tribe is a distinct sovereign, separate from the federal government and separate from the states.

The relationship between the tribes and the states can also be described as government-to-government. In the relations between tribes and states, persons representing states should remember that tribes are different from the states. The status of tribes has been described as that of "domestic dependent nations," and, as such, their sovereignty pre-dates the founding of the United States.[21]

As an example of how the government-to-government relationship is distinct and separate from public involvement obligations, the Unfunded Mandates Reform Act of 1995 provides that meetings between federal agency officials and "elected officers of state, local, and tribal governments (or their designated employees with authority to act on their behalf) acting in official capacities" are not subject to the Federal Advisory Committee Act [22] "where such meetings are solely for the purpose of exchanging views, information, or advice relating to the management or implementation of Federal programs ..."[23] The Tribal Caucus of the EPA Tribal Operations Committee is another group which fits within this exception.[24]

5. *Non-Federally Recognized Tribes*

There are indigenous communities who, although they existed prior to the formation of the United States, are not currently recognized as sovereigns by the federal government. State governments however, recognize some of these tribal communities as having a special political status within the state. Some of the indigenous communities, which are not recognized as having a special legal status, are currently engaged in seeking federal and/or state recognition.

Although such groups lack recognition as sovereigns, they may have environmental and public health concerns that are different from other groups or from the general public. These differences may exist due to a subsistence lifestyle and/or unique cultural practices. Agencies should seek to identify such groups and to include them in the decision-making processes. Although they do not have a unique political relationship with the federal government, non-federally recognized tribes may be comprised of "racial minorities" and therefore benefit from the full range of civil rights law protections.

6. *Indigenous Groups and Individual Tribal Members*

As citizens of the United States, tribal members (as individuals or representatives of indigenous organizations) have a right to environmental and public health protection under federal law comparable to that afforded to other citizens. Accordingly, individual tribal members and/or representatives from tribal organizations have a right to contact the federal government to express their environmental and public health concerns, whether such concerns arise on or off the reservation. Federal agencies must respond to such expressions of concern with the same respect that they afford other citizens and groups. Indeed, federal agencies should take affirmative steps to involve and communicate with individual tribal members and/or representatives from tribal organizations. Such affirmative efforts should often go beyond mere letter writing, and include opportunities for direct face to face contact (See Chapter 3, "Methods for Effective Communication").

B. Presidential Directives on Relations with Indian Tribes

To ensure that all federal agencies interact with tribes in a manner consistent with their sovereign status and their rights under federal law, the President has issued a number of directives to federal agencies. Some of these directives are summarized below.

1. Consultation and Coordination with Indian Tribal Governments

Executive Order 13084, Consultation and Coordination With Indian Tribal Governments, signed on May 14, 1998, directs federal agencies to respect tribal self-government and sovereignty, tribal rights, and tribal responsibilities whenever they formulate policies "significantly or uniquely affecting Indian tribal governments."[25] When developing regulatory policies, agencies should provide for "meaningful and timely" consultation with tribes, and must also consider the compliance costs imposed upon tribal governments. The Order further states: "On issues relating to tribal self-government, trust resources or treaty and other rights, each agency should explore and, where appropriate, use consensual mechanisms for developing regulations, including negotiated rule-making."

2. Government-to-Government Relations

On April 29, 1994, President Clinton executed a Presidential Memorandum outlining principles that executive agencies should follow in their interactions with tribal governments.[26] The purpose of the memorandum is to clarify the federal government's responsibility to operate within a government-to-government relationship with tribes. It directs agency heads to ensure that their agency personnel are familiar with the memorandum and that they comply with its requirements. The five main principles require agencies to:

(a)   Operate within a government-to-government relationship with tribes.

(b)   Consult, to the greatest extent practicable, with tribes prior to taking actions that affect tribes. These consultations must be open and candid so that all interested parties may determine the potential impact of proposed actions.

(c)   Assess the impact of all federal plans, projects, programs, and activities on tribal trust resources, and assure those tribes' rights and concerns are considered during the development of plans, projects, programs and activities.

(d)   Take appropriate steps to remove procedural impediments to working directly and effectively with tribes on activities affecting the property or rights of tribes.

(e)   Work cooperatively with other agencies to accomplish the goals of this memorandum.

The memorandum also directs agencies to apply the requirements of two other Executive Orders to address unique needs of tribes - Executive Orders No. 12875 "Enhancing the Intergovernmental Partnership"[27] and 12866 "Regulatory Planning and Review."[28]

3. Indian Sacred Sites

Executive Order 13007, Indian Sacred Sites (May 24, 1996), directs each federal agency that manages federal lands to "(1) accommodate access to and ceremonial use of Indian sacred sites by Indian religious practitioners and (2) avoid adversely affecting the physical integrity of such sacred sites." This executive order also directs each federal agency to report to the President on "procedures implemented or proposed to facilitate consultation with appropriate Indian tribes and religious leaders

4. *Environmental Justice*

Executive Order 12898, "Federal Actions to Address Environmental Justice in Minority Populations and Low-Income Populations," directs each federal agency to make achieving environmental justice part of its mission.[30] This executive order sets forth a number of responsibilities for federal agencies, including the requirements that each agency develop a strategy to identify and address "disproportionately high and adverse human health or environmental effects of its programs, policies, and activities on minority populations and low-income populations." In addition, section 6-606 of this executive order states: "Each Federal agency responsibility set forth under this order shall apply equally to Native American programs." This section also directs that the Department of the Interior, in coordination with the Working Group [established by the executive order], and, "after consultation with tribal leaders, shall coordinate steps to be taken pursuant to this order that address Federally recognized Indian tribes."

C.   EPA Policy on Environmental Programs on Indian Reservations

In 1984, EPA became one of the first federal agencies outside the Department of the Interior to adopt a formal policy statement on its relationship with Indian tribes and the implementation of its programs on Indian reservations. This EPA Policy, titled "Policy for the Administration of Environmental Programs on Indian Reservations"[31] (EPA 1984 Indian Policy), includes nine principles, some of which are particularly relevant to consultation with tribes. For example, principle 1 recognizes the government-to-government relationship and states that EPA "stands ready to work with Indian tribal governments on a one-to-one basis." Principle 2 recognizes that tribal governments are the "primary parties for setting standards, making environmental policy decisions and managing programs for reservations." Principle 5 acknowledges the federal trust responsibility and states that, in keeping with this responsibility, EPA will "assure that tribal concerns and interests are considered whenever EPA's actions and/or decisions may affect reservation environments." Principle 6 states that EPA will "encourage cooperation between tribal, state and local governments to resolve environmental problems of mutual concern." Principle 9 states that EPA will "incorporate these Indian Policy goals into its planning and management activities, including its budget. . . ." However, despite the EPA 1984 Indian Policy, federal funding for tribal environmental programs and environmental enforcement within Indian country has been inadequate and inequitable, particularly in light of the billions of federal dollars spent on state environmental efforts over the last three decades, although funding for tribal programs has increased substantially in recent years. Inadequate funding for tribal programs is considered by many to be an environmental justice issue, and is one of the key factors which impedes effective consultation with tribes due to the limited capacity of tribal environmental programs.

CHAPTER 2: WHAT CONSULTATION MEANS

Federal agencies use terms such as "public participation" and "consultation" to describe processes for facilitating public input and/or involvement in government decision-making. Other terms include "stakeholder involvement," "public-private partnerships," and "collaboration." When a federal agency works in a reciprocal way with one or more non-federal entities in fashioning a solution to a problem and in carrying out the solution, the term "collaboration" may be more accurate than "consultation." This is especially true in Indian country.

The terms represent points on a spectrum, from a minimal level of effort to inform the public about what a government agency is doing to providing genuine opportunities for affected individuals and groups to influence government decisions. In some cases, involvement in an agency decision may extend to participation in carrying out the decision. This may be particularly appropriate when an entity affected by the agency decision is itself a governmental entity, such as an Indian tribe. While these terms do not have standardized definitions and mean different things to different people, as discussed in this Chapter, in Indian country, consultation is a distinct concept.

A.   How Consultation Differs from Public Participation

Many federal statutes require government agencies to inform the public about their actions and to provide opportunities for concerned members of the public to express their views. For example, the Administrative Procedure Act requires all federal agencies to publish their proposed rules (also known as regulations) in the Federal Register and solicit comments from the public.[32] Only after having taken this step to solicit public involvement can a federal agency publish final rules that have the force of law. State agencies are subject to similar requirements under state law, and many tribal governments have imposed similar requirements on tribal agencies.

In addition to requirements imposed by statutes, rules issued by federal agencies can impose requirements to provide opportunities for public involvement. A leading example can be found in the rules issued by the Council on Environmental Quality to implement the National Environmental Policy Act (NEPA), which establish extensive requirements for public involvement in the preparation of environmental impact statements.[33]

Although there is no standard definition of "consultation," it generally does mean more than simply providing information about what an agency is planning to do and allowing concerned people to comment. Rather, "consultation" generally means that there must be two-way communication. In its guidelines for federal agency historic preservation programs, the National Park Service provides one definition of "consultation":

> "Consultation means the process of seeking, discussing, and considering the views
> of others, and, where feasible, seeking agreement with them on how historic
> properties should be identified, considered, and managed. Consultation is built
> upon the exchange of ideas, not simply providing information."[34]

This definition is also incorporated in the regulations of the Advisory Council on Historic Preservation dealing with consultation under Section 106 of the National Historic   Preservation Act.[35]

While consultation means more than simply providing information, it does not mean that the parties being consulted have the power to stop a federal agency action by withholding consent.[36] There may be instances in which a federal agency decides not to proceed with a proposed action as a result of consultation. In some instances another federal agency or a non-federal entity may have the legal authority to stop a proposed action. In other cases, however, consultation does not lead to an agreement, but rather ends when it becomes clear that an agreement will not be reached. In some situations in which a tribe does not have legal authority to prevent a federal agency from going forward with a proposed action, an agency nevertheless may decide not to proceed because to do so would jeopardize the existence of an ongoing consultative relationship with the tribe. Such a relationship could be jeopardized if, for example, an agency were to conclude consultation with a decision to allow development that would destroy a tribal sacred place or damage a biological community that tribal members use for traditional cultural practices. In such a situation, it could take years or even generations to rebuild a consultative relationship.

B. Affirmative Obligation of Federal Agencies to Consult with Tribes

A number of federal statutes, if not the federal-tribal trust relationship itself, require agencies to consult with tribes. Many of these statutes are summarized in Addendum A. Just what federal agencies are required to do by law depends on the wording of the particular statutes and regulations that apply to a given situation. Whatever the specific requirements, it must be stressed that federal agencies have affirmative obligations to seek out tribes and provide meaningful opportunities for consultation. This generally means much more than sending letters, notices, and copies of documents to tribes and requesting comment. Rather, there must be outreach and concerted efforts to provide for meaningful involvement in the decision-making processes.

C. Consultation in Addition to, Not Instead of, Public Participation

Consultation with tribal governments does not take the place of whatever requirements to promote public participation may apply to a given proposed federal action. The citizens of Indian country have the same kinds of rights to become involved in federal decision-making processes that citizens elsewhere have. Both consultation and public participation need to be viewed as ongoing obligations, which agencies should approach with creativity and cultural sensitivity. Although many public involvement opportunities tend to exist for a set period of time, consultation with the tribal government should continue on an ongoing basis.

D. The Goal of Consultation

The goal of any tribal consultation should be consensus, or in other words, full agreement between all of the parties involved in the consultation. Included within that goal, and where appropriate, federal agencies must be prepared to give tribal views deference when making decisions affecting tribal interests. Where, after a diligent and good faith effort has been made by the federal agency(ies) to achieve consensus, it is determined that consensus is not possible, then the federal agency(ies) should seek to achieve as substantial agreement as possible among those who are participating. In addition, the views of those not in agreement should be completely and fairly recorded in any document published by federal agency(ies) following the consultation. Finally, when the federal agency(ies) has completed its consultation process, or in good faith determined that further consultation would not be purposeful, it is important for the agency(ies) to issue its final decision expeditiously. By doing so, the federal agency(ies) timely advise those who participated in the consultation process how their views were taken into consideration. Where the federal agency(ies) decision concurs with tribal views, early decision making will help improve agency-tribal relations. On the other hand, where the federal agency's decision is contrary to tribal views, the tribe and its members are then on timely notice that specific steps may be required to pursue reconsideration or appeal of the decision.

E.   Accountability

All federal agency employees responsible for implementing, administering or supervising any aspect of tribal consultation must be held accountable for their responsibilities. One of the most effective ways to provide for accountability is for each agency to implement procedures for appeals to higher agency levels when it is believed that responsible agency personnel are not fulfilling their responsibilities with regard to consultation. In addition, agency managers should impress upon their staff the particular importance of consultation with tribes as compared to other groups or entities, and require that each staff member be fully aware of their responsibilities with regard to tribal consultation. Finally, agency managers themselves must remain open to reconsidering staff decisions related to tribal consultation in order to assure that the agency has fully complied with its responsibilities.

F.   Accommodating Tribal Rights and Federal Environmental Law (An Example)

On June 4, 1997, Interior Secretary Bruce Babbitt and Commerce Secretary William Daley signed a joint secretarial order that provides guidance to agencies on how to balance the interests of Indian tribes with requirements of the Endangered Species Act.[37] The order is an example of a federal policy that goes beyond simply including tribes in a consultative process in which tribal interests are considered. Rather, the order requires that tribal rights be prioritized in endangered species decisions. The order requires an equitable distribution of the burdens of protecting endangered species and directs agencies to "recognize that Indian tribes are appropriate governmental entities to manage their lands and tribal trust resources." (Principle 3B).[38]

CHAPTER 3: METHODS FOR EFFECTIVE CONSULTATION

This Chapter seeks to provide answers to the following questions: What does the tribe want to happen in consultation? When does a tribe feel like it was adequately consulted? This Chapter presents the views of the Indigenous Peoples Subcommittee on the guiding principles and critical elements for effective consultation with tribes. The mechanics and logistics of consultation can vary depending on a variety of factors, and some agencies have engaged in negotiations with tribes, often on a regional basis, to establish written protocols or agreements on how they will conduct consultation. In addition, some federal agencies have issued their own internal guidance documents on consultation with tribes, some of which are listed in Addendum.

A.   Guiding Principles

These guiding principles, which also are outlined in Addendum C, are designed to facilitate effective consultation and collaboration with tribes. While government contractors are encouraged to use these principles, federal agency officials ultimately are responsible for ensuring proper consultation with tribes. In applying these principles agency personnel must keep in mind the great diversity among tribes, and therefore be prepared to adapt these principles to any consultation or, with the consent of the tribe, develop additional principles. Government contractors should also use these principles, but agency officials should be aware that they are ultimately responsible for ensuring that proper consultation with tribes is carried out. Accordingly, federal agencies should follow these principles in developing and executing contracts.

1.   Know the tribes. In order for any effective consultation to take place, it is imperative that all federal agencies know of all of the tribes and tribal organizations, and the knowledgeable individual tribal members, within their jurisdiction. This includes not only tribes with jurisdiction over tribal land, but also those tribes, which claim a historical, cultural, religious, customary, cultural or aboriginal relationship with land within the agency's jurisdiction. Federal agency staff and managers should make every effort to identify all tribes and tribal organizations within their jurisdiction at the earliest possible time, and preferably before any consultation is commenced. Agencies also should identify tribes that may attach religious and cultural importance to historic places that may be affected by agency actions. In doing so, the agency should not rely on reservation boundary maps or census records, since these may not accurately reflect all tribes that have interests in a particular area.

2.   Build on-going consultative relationships with tribes. Consultation on specific proposed actions, policies, programs or other activities will be more constructive if conducted within the framework of an ongoing government-to-government relationship. In addition, since consultation puts demands on tribes as well as on agencies, the existence of on-going relationships will help tribes and agencies decide how to best allocate their resources among specific matters on which consultation may be appropriate.

3.   Institutionalize consultation and collaboration procedures. Agencies should work closely with tribes to develop formal consultation policies . Agency policy and procedures on consultation and collaboration with tribes should be published and made available to tribal governments and the affected public. However, specific arrangements with a particular tribe might be recorded in a memorandum of agreement or similar document which, although a public document, need not be widely distributed.

4. ***Contact tribes as early as practicable and allow sufficient time for the consultation process.*** This is necessary not only to allow a tribe to formulate and to express its views, but also for the agency to consider thoroughly the tribal views expressed before decision-making. In determining what is sufficient time for the tribal consultation process, agencies should not be driven by their own agendas or by their perceptions of the political climate. Rather, agency officials and staff should bear in mind the trust responsibility to each tribe and should try to schedule their consultation efforts so that the tribe will have meaningful opportunities to participate and will not be unduly burdened. If a tribe does not respond to an initial request to engage in consultation, the agency should not assume that the tribe has no interest in the matter. In such a case, the agency should pursue additional efforts to initiate tribal consultation. Based on the overall history of federal dealings with tribes, agencies should be cognizant that some tribal governments may well enter consultations questioning whether their participation will be meaningful.

5. ***Establish training programs for all staff on consultation with tribes.*** Staff training should explain the agency's policies and procedures as well as concepts such as the trust responsibility, government-to-government relationship, and tribal sovereignty. Agencies should provide frequent training on an ongoing basis with quality controls to ensure that the training is consistent with agency policy and procedures.

6. ***Maintain honesty and integrity in their consultation processes.*** This includes being candid and open with all available information that may help a tribe make an informed decision or take a position. It also means that tribal concerns are acknowledged and will be recorded for future reference. Respond in a timely manner to the tribal concerns prior to making decisions to demonstrate that the tribal input was meaningfully considered, and not disregarded.

7. **View tribal consultation as an integral and essential element of the government-to-government relationship with tribal governments, and not simply as a procedural requirement.** Agencies should view consultation as a non-adversarial opportunity to develop consensus solutions in partnership with tribal governments.

B.   Critical Elements

1.   *Preparation for consultation*

a. ***Be aware that tribes are culturally and administratively different from each other.*** Each tribal government is a unique and separate sovereign, with varying degrees of governmental infrastructure and financial and human resources. Accordingly, to the greatest extent possible, staff should be knowledgeable as to the governmental infrastructure and resources of each tribe. Although at times, tribes unite to express concerns over impacts to tribal sovereignty, jurisdiction, etc., their perspectives, positions, attitudes, and concerns can vary significantly.

b. ***Allow ample time for the tribe to receive, process, and respond to requests for consultation.*** The amount of time required for effective consultation will vary according to the particular tribe and in light of the complexity of the specific matter. Time frames for each step in the consultation process could be specified in written agreements between a tribe and the agency.

        c.   Understand that some kinds of information are sensitive, especially information regarding traditional religious practices. Tribes may be reluctant to divulge certain information unless confidentiality can be assured. In some instances, tribal customary law or religious rules regarding confidentiality are simply non-negotiable. Tribes also may require that an agency hold confidential proprietary information regarding their natural resources and economic development. The agency, however, must be careful not to overstate its ability to limit public access to sensitive information in light of the statutory requirements of the Freedom of Information Act.[39]

        d.   Steps of Consultation. It is beyond the scope of the Guide to provide a comprehensive and detailed step by step guide to consultation, particularly since the mechanics of consultation may vary from tribe to tribe. Nonetheless, participants in consultation should be aware that there are various federal publications which can provide more detailed guidance on consultation. Some of these publications are set forth in Addendum B. Additionally, refer to Addendum C for a list of some of the mechanics of consultation.

2.   *Participants in consultation and collaboration*

        a.   Tribal Contacts. Each tribe has the right to determine who will represent it in the consultation process. A tribe may have enacted legislation that identifies the specific tribal officials assigned the responsibilities for serving as the contact persons for certain kinds of consultation. Such responsibilities also may be assigned in tribal council resolutions. If a tribe has formally designated such contacts, agencies should work directly with them. If such persons have not been appointed, agencies should generally begin by contacting the chief executive officer of the tribe. If an agency enters into an agreement with a tribe to establish an on-going consultative relationship, the agreement should specify the tribal and agency persons who will serve as contacts.

        b.   Federal Government Interagency Working Groups. All tribal communities have dealings with several federal agencies, in a variety of contexts. These may include federal actions within reservation boundaries, federal actions outside reservation boundaries that have on-reservation effects, and actions that affect off-reservation places in which tribes have treaty rights or religious and cultural interests. Some tribes may prefer having federal agencies coordinate their consultation efforts to reduce the burden on tribal staff and other resources. Federal agencies with established contacts with a tribe may be helpful to other agencies that lack such contacts. Examples are:

- Five agency (EPA, BIA, IHS, USFS, HUD) MOU workgroup (EPA Region 5)
- BIA Area offices meeting with EPA Regional Administrators (EPA Region 6)
- EPA Tribal Operations Committee (TOC)
- EPA Regional Tribal Operations Committees (RTOC)

        c.   Inter-Tribal Organizations. For policy development affecting many tribes, consult and engage national tribal organizations such as the National Congress of American Indians (NCAI), National Tribal Environmental Council (NTEC), and Native American Fish and Wildlife Society (NAFWS). For issues of regional scope, consultation with regional inter-tribal organizations may be appropriate. In light of the fact that each tribe has a government-to-government relationship with the United States, use of inter-tribal organizations generally should emphasize facilitating communication between agencies and the tribes that comprise the organization. Under no circumstance should an agency treat consultation with inter-tribal organizations as a substitute for consultation with each tribe, unless the tribes comprising such an organization agree that consultation should proceed through an inter-tribal organization. However, some tribes may direct that all consultation begin with inter-tribal organizations. Regional offices of the agencies usually know and can identify these relationships.

> **d.** *Traditional Religious Leaders and Cultural Authorities.* In some instances, it may be advisable for agencies to seek information from tribal members in addition to persons who have been formally designated by tribal governments as contacts for consultation. For example, in the context of the Native American Graves Protection and Repatriation Act (NAGPRA),[40] federal agencies have an obligation to seek to identify traditional religious leaders who should be consulted (although the NAGPRA regulations recognize that input from religious leaders may be provided through tribal governmental officials). In the context of the National Historic Preservation Act (NHPA),[41] federal agencies should seek information on traditional cultural places from elders and other persons who have knowledge of such places. Agencies should not be surprised to learn that the interests of traditional leaders and cultural authorities do not always coincide with those of the tribal government.

3. *Logistics and Mechanics*

> **a.** *Protocol.* In recognition of the government-to-government relationship, agencies should, unless otherwise directed by the tribe, ensure interaction through officials of comparable governmental stature and authority. It is important to know that tribal leaders are of the highest levels of tribal government stature and should be treated in like manner. Federal agencies should strive to consult with tribal Chief Executive Officers through the agencies' regional directors or officials of similar stature.

> **b.** *Staff contacts.* Agencies should strive to establish staff level relations to complement contacts by governmental officials. Use phone calls, meetings, e-mail, and other means of communication to maintain such relations, which can be more beneficial to tribes than manuals or formal policies. Do not expect tribal staff to make policy decisions, however, or to take tribal positions without authorization from their tribal governments.

> **c.** *Two-way communication.* The goal of consultation, both that at the level of governmental officials and at the staff level, should be direct, two-way dialogue. Seek face-to-face meetings at tribal offices. These meetings will develop rapport and increase understanding of the proposed action as well as outline the agency's perceived constraints (on the decision under consideration and on the resources it can devote to consultation). Where the focus of the consultation is a specific site or location, agency personnel should arrange to visit the site or location with tribal representatives so as to achieve the best possible understanding of the tribe's concerns. In addition to face-to-face meetings, agencies should maintain an on-going dialogue through telephone calls, written correspondence, and other methods of communication.

> **d.** *Clear description of the proposed action or policy.* Documents and

statements should clearly describe the proposed action or policy to tribal representatives and community members. Explain in plain and simple terms what the agency wants to accomplish, where the agency is in its decision making, and the nature of the decision to be made. Limit the use of confusing acronyms when consulting with tribal government officials, but if they must be used, include a clear definition of their meanings.

　　　　　e. 　　　***Informational meetings for larger audiences.*** Invite tribal contacts to attend or co-sponsor public meetings regarding proposed actions. "Piggy-back" informational meetings with scheduled tribal public functions to reach larger audiences. Allow plenty of time for discussion and explanation of technical details, and give the affected community the opportunity to provide the agency with well-informed input. Informational meetings should not be used to replace separate agency meetings with tribal leadership, which is an essential element of consultation.

　　　　　f. 　　　***Public involvement.*** For proposed actions and policies in which it is appropriate to seek involvement from members of the affected public, consult with tribes about how to do so effectively. Agencies may be able to use a tribal newspaper, radio station, or tribal information network to publicize outreach activities.

　　　　　g. 　　　***Outcomes of consultation.*** The outcome of consultation is different than the goal for consultation. Whereas the goal of consultation pertains to the scope of agreement, the outcome of consultation addresses what is to be agreed upon. In this regard it is important for the federal agency to share with tribes a range of consultation outcomes not only from the agency's perspective, but also the tribal perspective. Agencies should ask tribal representatives to identify the ultimate goals of the consultation and be open to those suggestions.

CHAPTER FOUR: PUBLIC PARTICIPATION IN INDIAN COUNTRY

A.   Why Public Participation is Important for all Governments

Public participation is a valuable function of government. It provides important information upon which government officials may base their decisions affecting the public. This is particularly important in the design and implementation of environmental and public health programs. Government officials may not understand how some individuals or groups bear disproportionate impacts unless the public has the opportunity to express its concerns. By affording individuals and groups the opportunity to speak for themselves, government agencies can base decisions on more accurate information. This may help create a sense of ownership with the public groups, lead to community support for government action, and assure environmental justice.

Meaningful public participation is a fundamental principle of environmental justice. The EPA Office of Environmental Justice defines Environmental Justice as:

> The fair treatment and meaningful involvement of all people regardless of race, color, national origin, or income with respect to the development, implementation, and enforcement of environmental laws, regulations, and policies. Fair treatment means that no group of people, including racial, ethnic, or socioeconomic group should bear a disproportionate share of the negative environmental consequences resulting from industrial, municipal, and commercial operations or the execution of federal, state, local, and tribal programs and policies.[42]

B.   Public Participation in EPA's Programs

As noted in earlier chapters, the federal government has a particular set of responsibilities to federally recognized tribal governments. These responsibilities extend well beyond the call for federal agencies to provide opportunities for tribal governments to participate in decision-making processes as part of the affected public. Rather, the working relationships that need to exist between the federal and tribal governments should be consultative and collaborative. These responsibilities to consult with tribes, however, are separate from federal agency responsibilities to provide opportunities for individual members of the public and non-governmental organizations to have input into agency decisions that affect them. Thus, while agencies such as EPA are required to work with tribes on a government-to-government basis, this does not diminish an agency's obligation to be responsive to individual citizens.

As a federal agency, the EPA is subject to federal laws intended to make agencies accountable to the public, such as the Administrative Procedure Act (APA).[43] The APA establishes the basic requirements for two kinds of activities that governmental agencies carry out: (1) rule-making, through which agencies implement legislation; and (2) administrative adjudication, through which agencies make decisions that affect particular individuals. Rule-making is one of the basic ways through which agencies seek public input into the development of policies. Rule-making, as carried out by federal agencies, typically involves publication of rules in proposed form for public review and comment. Rule-making may also include legislative-style hearings in which members of the public are invited to express their view. Administrative adjudication includes the issuance of permits and licenses, and appeals regarding such decisions. For adjudication, the APA sets out the standards to ensure that the government agency provides due process to all persons who are subject to its decisions. The APA also sets out the standards for federal courts to use when agency actions are challenged.

When EPA engages in rule-making or adjudication, it must comply with the requirements of the APA, as well as any additional requirements that are included in the statutes that EPA is charged with carrying out. In accordance with these laws, EPA has issued several sets of regulations that govern public involvement in EPA programs.[44] As a general rule, the requirements of such regulations apply to EPA when the Agency administers environmental regulatory programs within Indian reservations or in Alaska Native villages, separately and in addition to the duties of EPA to consult with tribal governments. In general, federal agencies are required to treat the concerns of a tribal member in the same manner as any citizen of the United States.

EPA must make reasonable efforts to inform and seek participation from tribal members, organizations, and communities about the Agency's actions and programs in a manner similar to the way the Agency works with other citizens, non-governmental organizations, and communities. Specifically, interested tribal members, tribal community groups, and tribal non-governmental organizations need to be invited to attend public meetings on proposed actions or policies that may affect their communities. Providing opportunities for public participation helps to build a record for an informed decision. These individuals, groups, and organizations need to also be provided with information about EPA's newsletters, financial assistance programs, and employment opportunities. In addition, it may be appropriate for such individuals to be appointed to serve on federal advisory committees (as representatives of non-governmental organizations) or for such organizations to participate in identifying supplemental environmental projects (which arise from litigation concerning their communities).

When environmental and public health concerns arise within or near Indian country and Alaska Native villages, concerned citizens and groups   whether Indian or non-Indian   may contact EPA or another federal agency for information and help. When such situations arise, federal agencies must respond to the concerns of individuals or groups in ways that are respectful of tribal sovereignty, the government-to-government relationship, and the federal trust responsibility. Consultation with the tribal government can, and generally should, be carried out before, during and after federal efforts are made to address these concerns. This appears to be consistent with one of the key principles of the EPA 1984 Indian Policy, which states that EPA "will recognize tribal governments as the primary parties for … making environmental policy decisions … for reservations, consistent with agency standards and regulations."

The EPA 1984 Indian Policy specifically addresses the situation in which a regulated facility on a reservation that is not owned or operated by the tribal government is out of compliance with federal environmental law, and the tribal government has not taken over primary enforcement authority. In such cases, EPA will seek to act in cooperation with the affected tribal government but will generally respond to noncompliance by private parties "as the Agency would respond to noncompliance elsewhere in the country."[45] The involvement of concerned citizens can be useful in bringing such cases to the attention of EPA. As it works to bring the facility into compliance, the Agency should generally seek to address all concerns about human health and the environment, regardless of who initially raises such concerns. If such enforcement efforts lead to settlement agreements that include any supplemental environmental projects (SEPs), input and support from the tribal government and the community(ies) affected by the non-compliance should be sought in the design of the SEPs.

The EPA 1984 Indian Policy also addresses the situation in which tribally owned or managed facility is out of compliance with federal environmental law. As with privately owned facilities, the involvement of concerned citizens can be useful in bringing such cases to the attention of EPA. The EPA 1984 Indian Policy favors cooperation with the tribal government, with technical assistance and consultation, to bring such a facility into compliance. Administrative and judicial enforcement processes will generally not be used unless there is a significant threat to human health or the environment and enforcement is the only way to correct the problem in a timely fashion.

C.   Public Participation in Tribal Environmental Programs

Increasingly, tribal governments are called upon to address important social, cultural, religious/spiritual, economic, public health, and environmental issues affecting their lands and the people (both tribal members and non-members) residing on or near reservations. Tribal leaders may be driven to act by their own awareness of these issues. They may also act in response to concerns voiced by tribal members, non-member Indians, non-Indians, businesses, and community organizations. The need for governmental action may be brought to the attention of tribal leaders by officials of other tribes or federal, state, or local governments. For these and other reasons, tribal leaders are increasingly recognizing that sovereignty includes responsibility for environmental protection.

As the number of tribes assuming responsibility for environmental protection grows, tribal governments are being asked to provide greater access to their decision-making processes. Tribes that assume regulatory roles under federal statutes also become subject to certain public participation requirements imposed by federal laws and regulations. EPA regulations impose a range of requirements for public participation and due process on state regulatory programs operated within the framework of federal law, and many of these requirements apply to tribes that become authorized for treatment in the same manner as states.[46]

Providing for public participation in the tribal government context, however, presents unusual considerations. In the first place, tribes have the right of self-government as an integral aspect of tribal sovereignty, and this includes the right to determine the structure, nature, and functions of that government. As a result, each tribal government is unique, and the processes by which tribal members participate vary from tribe to tribe. For example, in some tribes, a general council consisting of every tribal member entitled to vote comprises the tribal governing body. In such cases, much discussion and broad participation typically occurs during tribal decision making. Other tribes have established a smaller governing body, such as an elected or appointed tribal council and/or executive committee, which may exercise a broad range of authorities on behalf of the tribe. Some tribes have governing bodies that carry on ancient tribal traditions. Many tribal governments reflect a mix of tribal traditions and American democratic government.

The extent to which the institutions of tribal government provide for involvement of tribal members, whether through formal processes or customary practices, is largely a matter for the people of each tribe to decide for themselves. On many reservations, however, there are many people living and doing business who are not tribal members. Such demographic factors may raise special public participation challenges concerning the extent and process by which non-Indian and non-member Indian reservation residents may have a say in tribal decisions affecting the environment and public health, whether or not such persons share in the tribe's value system. The presence of substantial numbers of non-Indians within reservations, many of whom are landowners, is part of the legacy of the "allotment" era of federal Indian policy, which the federal government repudiated in 1934. Between 1887, when the General Allotment Act was passed, and 1934, when it was ended by the Indian Reorganization Act, the allotment policy resulted in about two-thirds of Indian land passing out of Indian possession.[47] Because a checkerboard system of regulating environmental quality is unworkable, many tribes have sought to exercise regulatory authority over their entire reservations, including non-Indian lands and activities, and EPA has generally supported such efforts. In some cases, EPA's support for tribal authority over non-Indians has been challenged in court.[48]

In light of such factors, mechanisms to enhance public participation in tribal government decision-making may be helpful, if not essential, for tribal environmental programs to gain acceptance. Moreover, unless tribes provide for meaningful public involvement, it is quite likely tribes will face continuous challenges to their governmental authority in the federal courts and state and federal political arenas. It is therefore essential that EPA and other federal agencies work with tribes, in a government-to-government way, to help them develop appropriate public participation processes that not only comply with any applicable federal requirements, but also will complement existing tribal structure, laws, and practices.

Federal agency efforts to help tribes develop public participation processes may be pursued in a proactive way, or such efforts may be initiated in response to concerns raised by individuals or groups in particular matters. Where a tribe is asserting regulatory authority over its entire reservation, it is likely that some individuals or community-based organizations may disagree or complain about tribal actions. Federal agencies should recognize that, as is the case throughout society, not all people agree with government decisions, whether those decisions are made by federal, tribal, state, or local governments.

One promising approach to addressing this problem is for tribal governments to enact and enforce administrative procedure acts (APAs). As discussed earlier in this Chapter, the federal APA, sets the standards for two kinds of activities that governmental agencies carry out: (1) rule-making, through which agencies implement legislation and may seek input from all sectors of the affected public; and (2) administrative adjudication, through which agencies make decisions that affect particular individuals. About two-thirds of the states have enacted such legislation. Although a number of tribes have enacted such laws, most tribes have not.

In setting out the standards for administrative adjudication, a tribal APA can ensure that tribal agencies afford due process to permit applicants and other persons affected by permit decisions and administrative enforcement actions. The Indian Civil Rights Act (ICRA)[49] provides, in part, that no tribal government shall deny any person within its jurisdiction the equal protection of its laws or deprive any person of liberty or property without due process of law. The ICRA, however, does not provide a right of action in federal court unless a person is being held in custody,[50] a situation that generally does not apply to administrative agencies. (Many tribal courts have ruled that ICRA does create a right of action in tribal court.[51]) A tribal APA can provide specificity for the concept of due process as applied by tribal agencies. By doing so, a tribal APA can give members of the public the sense that they are being treated with fundamental fairness, which is a basic value in American democracy. In addition, an APA can expressly provide for jurisdiction in tribal courts to resolve claims by individuals that tribal agencies have not treated them with due process or have otherwise not complied with the law.

D.   How to Provide for Effective Public Participation

The National Environmental Justice Advisory Council (NEJAC) has recognized the crucial need for public participation particularly in the area of environmental justice. A guidance plan for public participation was created by the NEJAC, The Model Plan for Public Participation, and includes guiding principles, critical elements, and core values. This plan has been redrafted for the purposes of making it more applicable to Indian country. The title of this redraft is, "Public Participation Guiding Principles and Critical Elements," and can be found at the end of this document as Addendum D.

CONCLUSION

An intent of Indigenous Peoples Subcommittee in writing this Guide has been to familiarize readers with the concepts of American Indian and Alaska Native tribal sovereignty, and the resulting government-to-government relationship with the federal government. The Guide has provided, information on the legal requirements for such a relationship, and has offered guidelines on how to achieve such a relationship. The Guide has provided not only the legal requirements for such a relationship, but also guidelines on how to achieve such a relationship. Additionally, the Guide has defined the differences between public participation and consultation and collaboration, and when each communication technique is appropriate to use.

The Indigenous Peoples Subcommittee recognizes the strides that EPA has made in addressing environmental justice for American Indians and Alaska Natives. Through this document, NEJAC urges EPA to enhance its efforts to promote equity in environmental protection within Indian country and Alaska Native villages. Specifically, the Subcommittee calls on EPA to consult with tribal governments on a government-to-government basis, consistent with and in recognition of tribal sovereignty, tribal rights, and the federal trust responsibility. Additionally, it is imperative that EPA and other federal agencies afford federally recognized tribal governments with equitable levels of financial and technical assistance to ensure that public health, the environment and tribal cultural, spiritual, natural and economic resources are indeed protected from environmental degradation and harm.

Finally, the Indigenous Peoples Subcommittee requests that EPA encourage and assist tribal governments in establishing their environmental programs in an effective and open manner and administering their environmental laws and policies fairly and efficiently. Again, equitable levels of federal financial and technical assistance will be essential to strengthening and maintaining the overall integrity of tribal environmental programs. In the Subcommittee's view, strong, fair and successful tribal environmental programs not only will benefit tribal communities and their neighbors, but also will strengthen tribal sovereignty and self-governance and promote the acceptance of these bedrock principles throughout the larger American society.

ENDNOTES

[1] *See* Dept of the Interior, Secretarial Order 3206, American Indian Tribal Rights, Federal-Tribal Trust Responsibilities and the Endangered Species Act, June 5, 1997, available at http://endangered.fws.gov/esatribe.html.

[2] Worcester v. Georgia, 31 U.S. (6 Pet.) 515 (1832).

[3] *See* United States v. Wheeler, 435 U.S. 313 (1978), citing Oliphant v. Suquamish Indian Tribe, 435 U.S. 191 (1978), the first case in which the Court used the implicit divestiture theory to reach it holding.

[4] *See* N. Bruce Duthu, *Implicit Divestiture of Tribal Powers: Locating Legitimate Sources of Authority in Indian Country*, 19 AM. INDIAN L. REV. 353 (1994) (analyzing the use of the implicit divestiture by the Supreme Court to create a new theory of "judicial plenary power"); Frank Pommersheim, *Coyote Paradox: Some Indian Law Reflections from the Edge of the Prairie*, 31 ARIZ. ST. L. J. 439 (1999) (discussing the use of the new judicial plenary power doctrine in divesting tribes of sovereign powers); David H. Getches, *Conquering the Cultural Frontier: The New Subjectivism of the Supreme Court in Indian Law*, 84 CAL. L. REV. 1573 (1996) (explaining how the Supreme Court has used the implicit divestiture doctrine to reach results that reflect the Court's views of what the law ought to be).

[5] *See* Executive Memorandum on Government-to-Government Relations with Native American Tribal Governments (April 29, 1994).

[6] Seminole Nation v. United States, 316 U.S. 286, 297 (1942).

[7] Nance v. Environmental Protection Agency, 645 F.2d 701, 710 (9th Cir. 1981).

[8] United States v. Payne, 264 U.S. 446, 448 (1924).

[9] *See* United States v. Mitchell, 463 U.S. 206 (1983). In Mitchell, the Court found that the Department of the Interior was liable for monetary damages for mismanaging timber resources of the Quinault tribe in violation of the agency's fiduciary duty.

[10] 25 U.S.C. § 3601.

[11] *See* Morongo Band of Mission Indians v. Federal Aviation Admin., 161 F.3d 569, 574 (9th Cir. 1998) (recognizing the distinction between general and specific trust responsibilities).

[12] *See* Mary Christina Wood, *Protecting the Attributes of Native Sovereignty: A New Paradigm for Federal Actions Affecting Tribal Lands and Resources*, 1995 Utah L. Rev. 109, 117-21 (1995) (collecting cases and arguing that "[i]nterpreting governmental fiduciary standards as coextensive with express statutory obligations in general laws is inappropriate"). *See also* Mary Christina Wood, *Indian Land and the Promise of Native Sovereignty: The Trust Doctrine Revisited*, 1994 Utah L. Rev. 1471, 1513-1522 (1994) (discussing the U.S. Supreme Court's decisions in Mitchell v. United States, 445 U.S. 535 (1980) and Mitchell v. United States, 463 U.S. 206 (1983); noting that the reason the Court insisted on a specific basis in the "Constitution, statutes, federal regulations, executive orders, or treaties" as a requirement for finding the federal government liable for breach of trust is that these cases involved claims for damages under the Tucker Act, 28 U.S.C. § 1491, and the Indian Claims Commission Act, 28 U.S.C. § 1505; and arguing that this rationale should not be extended to claims for declaratory and/or injunctive relief under the Administrative Procedure Act, 5 U.S.C. § 702).

[13] *See* Morton v. Mancari, 417 U.S. 535 (1974).

[14] *See* McClanahan v. Arizona State Tax Comm., 411 U.S. 164 (1973) ("The policy of leaving Indians free from state jurisdiction is deeply rooted in the Nation's history.").

[15] *See Mancari*, 417 U.S. at 555.

[16] *See* Washington v. Washington State Commercial Passenger Fishing Vessel Assoc., 443 U.S. 658, 675 (1979).

[17] *See* United States v. Winans, 198 U.S. 371 (1905) ("In other words, the treaty was not a grant of rights to the Indians, but a grant of rights from them—a reservation of those not granted.")

[18] *See* Menominee Tribe of Indians v. United States, 391 U.S. 404 (1968).

[19] *See* United States v. Dion, 476 U.S. 734 (1986).

[20] *See* Oneida Indian Nation v. County of Oneida, 414 U.S. 661, 667-70 (1974).

[21] Cherokee Nation v. Georgia, 30 U.S. (6 pet.) 1 (1831).

[22] 5 U.S.C. App. 2 (1994).

[23] 2 U.S.C. § 1534.

[24] In order to improve communication and build stronger partnerships with the Tribes, the U.S. Environmental Protection Agency (EPA) established a Tribal Operations Committee in February 1994. The Tribal Operations Committee (TOC) is comprised of 19 Tribal leaders or their Environmental Program Managers (referred to as the

"Tribal Caucus") and EPA's Senior Leadership Team, including the Administrator, the Deputy Administrator and the Agency's Assistant Administrators and Regional Administrators. The Tribal Caucus (TC) meets on a regular basis to discuss implementation of the environmental protection programs for which EPA and the Tribes share responsibility as co-regulators. All Tribes are encouraged to communicate with the members of the TC.

[25] Exec. Order No. 13084, 63 Fed. Reg. 27,655 (May 14, 1998), reprinted in 25 U.S.C.A. § 450 note.

[26] Presidential Memorandum on Government-to Government Relationships, 59 Fed. Reg. 22,951 (April 29, 1998), reprinted in 25 U.S.C.A. § 450 note.

[27] Exec. Order No. 12875, 58 Fed. Reg. 58, 093 (Oct. 26, 1993).

[28] Exec. Order No. 12866, 58 Fed. Reg. 51,735 (Sept. 30, 1993).

[29] Exec. Order No. 13007, 61 Fed. Reg. 26771 (May 29, 1996), reprinted in 42 U.S.C. § 1996 note.

[30] Exec. Order No. 12898, 59 Fed. Reg. 7629 (Feb. 11, 1994).

[31] Environmental Protection Agency, EPA Policy for the Administration of Environmental Programs on Indian Reservations (Nov. 8, 1984), posted at <www.epa.gov/indian/1984.htm> (visited October 8, 2000).

[32] See 5 U.S.C. § 552 (1994).

[33] 42 U.S.C. §§ 4321-4370d.

[34] 63 Fed. Reg. 20,504 (April 24, 1998).

[35] See 36 C.F.R. § 800.15(f).

[36] See, e.g., Hoopa Valley Tribe v. Christie, 812 F.2d 1097 (9th Cir. 1986). "Consultation is not the same as obeying those who are consulted. The Hupas were heard, even though their advice was not accepted." Id. at 1103. But see Oglala Sioux Tribe of Indians v. Andrus, 603 F.2d 707 (8th Cir. 1979) (failure of agency to follow consultation guidelines violates trust obligation to tribe).

[37] Department of the Interior, supra note 1.

[38] Specifically, the order requires that agencies:

> . . . shall give deference to tribal conservation and management plans for tribal trust resources that: (a) govern activities on Indian lands, including . . . tribally-owned fee lands, and (b) address the conservation needs of listed species. The Departments shall conduct government-to-government consultations to discuss the extent to which tribal resource management plans for tribal trust resources outside Indian lands can be incorporated into actions to address the conservation needs of listed species. (Principle 3B).

When the Fish and Wildlife Service or the National Marine Fisheries Service determines that conservation restrictions are necessary to protect a species, the agency must again show that it is equitably distributing the burden of protecting a species. To meet this burden, an agency must notify a tribe of the restriction and show that the following conservation standards have been met:

> (i) the restriction is reasonable and necessary for conservation of the species at issue; (ii) the conservation purpose of the restriction cannot be achieved by reasonable regulation of non-Indian activities; (iii) the measure is the least restrictive alternative available to achieve the required conservation purpose; (iv) the restriction does not discriminate against Indian activities, either as stated or applied; and (v) voluntary tribal measures are not adequate to achieve the necessary conservation purpose. (Principle C3).

This Order provides important guidance to agencies on policies implementing the Endangered Species Act. It prioritizes the interests of Indian tribes in conserving species and in planning for economic development of Indian lands.

[39] 5 U.S.C. § 552(b). The Ninth Circuit has held that the trust doctrine does not necessarily shield agencies from FOIA requests for documents given to the agency by a tribe. See Klamath Water Users Assoc. v. United States Dept. of the Interior, 189 F.3d 1034, 1038-39 (9th Cir. 1999).

[40] See 25 U.S.C. §§ 3001-3013 (1994).

[41] See 16 U.S.C. §§ 470-470x-6.

[42] U.S. EPA, INTERIM FINAL GUIDANCE FOR INCORPORATING ENVIRONMENTAL JUSTICE CONCERNS IN EPA'S NEPA COMPLIANCE ANALYSIS 2 (Sept. 1997).

[43] 5 U.S.C. §§ 551-559, 701-706.

[44] *See, e.g.*, 40 C.F.R. Part 25, Public Participation in Programs under the Resource Conservation and Recovery Act, the Safe Drinking Water Act, and the Clean Water Act. See also 40 C.F.R. Part 124, Procedures for Decisionmaking (including numerous provisions relating to public notice, public comments, and hearings).

[45] *Id.*, Principle 8.

[46] *See, e.g.*, 40 C.F.R. Part 25, Public Participation in Programs under the Resource Conservation and Recovery Act, the Safe Drinking Water Act, and the Clean Water Act. The regulations in Part 25 apply to EPA programs, and some of these regulations apply to state programs under these three statutes. Although Part 25 does not mention tribes, some of the regulations in this Part do apply to tribes. For example, tribes that have been authorized for treatment in the same manner as a state for the purpose of setting water quality standards (WQSs) are subject to the requirement to hold a public hearing in accordance with Part 25 before adopting or revising their WQSs. 40 C.F.R. §§ 131.3(j), 131.20(b). *See generally* Dean B. Suagee and John P. Lowndes, *Due Process and Public Participation in Tribal Environmental Programs*, 13 TULANE ENVTL. L. J. 1, 25-41 (1999). Not all requirements imposed on states apply to tribes. For example, although tribes that apply for eligibility for the section 402 permit program under the Clean Water Act (also known as the National Pollutant Discharge Elimination System, or NPDES, permit program) are generally subject to the requirements for state programs, 40 C.F.R. § 123.31(b), the requirement to provide judicial review of the approval or denial of a NPDES permit does not apply to tribes. 40 C.F.R. § 123.30.

[47] *See generally* FELIX S. COHEN'S HANDBOOK OF FEDERAL INDIAN LAW (1982, Rennard Strickland, ed.); *see also* Judith V. Royster, *The Legacy of Allotment*, 27 ARIZ. ST. L. J. 1 (1995).

[48] E.g., Montana v. U.S. Environmental Protection Agency, 941 F. Supp. 945 (D. Mont. 1996), *aff'd*. 137 F.3d 1135 (9th Cir. 1998), *cert. denied*, 119 S.Ct. 275 (1998) (upholding EPA approval of tribal water quality standards for all surface waters within tribe's reservation); Arizona Public Service Company v. Environmental Protection Agency, 211 F.3d 1280, No. 98-1196, 2000 WL 493047 (D.C. Cir. 2000) (upholding EPA's determination that, in the 1990 Clean Air Act Amendments, Congress had delegated to tribes the authority to regulate all sources of air pollution within the boundaries of their reservations, including lands owned in fee by non-Indians).

[49] 25 U.S.C. §§ 1301-1303.

[50] Santa Clara Pueblo v. Martinez, 436 U.S. 49, 58, 66-67 (1978).

[51] *See* Robert J. McCarthy, *Civil Rights in Tribal Courts: The Indian Bill of Rights at Thirty Years*, 34 IDAHO L. REV. 465 (1998) (discussing tribal court case law construing the meaning of due process under ICRA).

STATUTES AND REGULATIONS

National Environmental Policy Act
42 U.S.C. §§ 4321-4370d

The National Environmental Policy Act (NEPA) requires the preparation of an environmental impact statement (EIS) for any proposed major federal action that may significantly affect the quality of the human environment. Under regulations issued by the Council of Environmental Quality (CEQ), 40 C.F.R. pts. 1500 1508, a federal agency may prepare a less-detailed document known as an environmental assessment (EA) for use in determining whether a proposed action may result in significant impacts on the environment. If the responsible agency official determines that the proposed action will not have significant impacts, a finding of no significant impact (FONSI) completes the NEPA process. If the EA does not support a FONSI, then an EIS must be prepared, unless new alternatives and/or mitigation measures are fashioned that will avoid significant impacts. In practice, for the vast majority of federal actions, an EA and FONSI fulfills the agency's responsibilities for NEPA compliance.

Although the statutory language of NEPA does not mention Indian tribes, the CEQ regulations require agencies to contact Indian tribes and provide opportunities for tribes to be become involved at several steps in the preparation of an EIS, including:

Cooperating agencies When the effects of a proposed action may occur "on a reservation" an Indian tribe, by agreement with the lead federal agency, may become a cooperating agency and have a direct role in the preparation of the EIS. 40 C.F.R. §§ 1501.6, 1508.5.

Scoping The lead agency must invite "any affected Indian tribe" to participate in the scoping process for an EIS. *Id.* § 1501.7.

Commenting on an EIS The lead agency must invite comments on a draft EIS from Indian tribes "when the effects may be on a reservation." *Id.* § 1503.1(a)(2).

Environmental consequences When an agency prepares an EIS for a proposed action, the analysis of environmental consequences in the EIS must include discussions of possible conflicts between the proposed action and the objectives of Federal, regional, State, and local (and in the case of a reservation, Indian tribe) land use plans, policies and controls for the area concerned. *Id.* § 1502.16(c).

Public involvement Whenever an agency provides public notice of a NEPA-related hearing, public meeting, or the availability of environmental documents, the notice shall include notice to Indian tribes "when effects may occur on reservations." *Id.* § 1506.6(b)(3).

In the event that an EA is prepared for a proposed federal action rather than an EIS, the CEQ regulations provide guidance on how to prepare the EA, either in terms of procedure or content. An

EA must include "brief discussions of the need for the proposal, of alternatives as required by section 102(2)(E) [of NEPA], of the environmental impacts of the proposed action and alternatives, and a listing of agencies and persons consulted." *Id.* § 1508.9. The agency "shall involve environmental agencies, applicants, and the public, to the extent practicable" in preparing EAs. *Id.* § 1501.4(b). The agency needs to determine if the action under review *may* "significantly" impact the quality of human health and the environment. *Id.* § 1508.27. If the agency issues a finding of no significant impact (FONSI) for a proposed action (i.e., determines that an EIS is not required), the agency must make the FONSI available to the public. *Id.* §§ 1501.4(e)(1), 1506.6. Agencies generally have broad discretion to do more than just what is needed to comply with these minimal requirements.

In addition, if the proposed federal agency action is in response to an action planned by a private or other non-federal entity, and the federal agency knows that its involvement is reasonably foreseeable, the CEQ regulations direct federal agencies to promptly consult with state and local agencies and Indian tribes. *Id.* § 1501.2(d). This requirement applies whether NEPA compliance involves an EIS or and EA and FONSI.

National Historic Preservation Act
16 U.S.C. §§ 470 470x-6

Section 106 of the National Historic Preservation Act (NHPA) requires each federal agency to take into account the effect of any proposed federal or federally assisted undertaking on places that are listed on or eligible for listing on the National Register of Historic Places, and to give the Advisory Council on Historic Preservation (ACHP) an opportunity to comment on any such undertaking. This review requirement, which is known as the Section 106 consultation process, is governed by regulations issued by the ACHP. 36 C.F.R. pt. 800. The ACHP regulations were recently published as revised final rules. 64 Fed. Reg. 27044 (May 18, 1999). The revised final rules implement amendments to the NHPA enacted in 1992. Under the ACHP regulations, the federal agency typically carries out the section 106 process in consultation with the appropriate State Historic Preservation Officer (SHPO), and the ACHP only becomes directly involved in unusual cases.

Places that hold religious and cultural significance for Indian tribes, or for Native Hawaiian organizations, may be eligible for the National Register. Such places may be eligible for the National Register because of their ongoing importance in the cultural beliefs and practices of a tribe or Native Hawaiian community. Such places are often called "traditional cultural properties" or "traditional cultural places" (TCPs). *See generally* NATIONAL PARK SERVICE, NATIONAL REGISTER BULLETIN 38, GUIDELINES FOR EVALUATING AND DOCUMENTING TRADITIONAL CULTURAL PROPERTIES (1990).

The 1992 NHPA Amendments enacted new statutory provisions relating to Indian tribes and Native Hawaiian organizations:

Indian tribes can choose to take over the functions of the SHPO for "tribal lands," a term that is defined in the NHPA to include all lands within the exterior boundaries of any Indian reservation and all dependent Indian communities. NHPA § 101(d)(2); 16 U.S.C. § 470a(d)(2).

If a proposed federal or federally assisted undertaking may affect a historic property that a tribe or Native Hawaiian organization (NHO) regards as holding religious and cultural significance, the federal agency has a statutory obligation to consult with the tribe or NHO as part of the Section 106 process. NHPA § 101(d)(6); 16 U.S.C. § 470a(d)(6).

Under the revised regulations, the Section 106 process will usually consist of four steps. The federal agency that is considering the proposed undertaking is responsible for taking each step, in consultation with the appropriate state historic preservation officer (SHPO) or tribal historic preservation officer (THPO) and other consulting parties.

Step 1 – Initiate the Section 106 Process. The federal agency official determines whether the proposed federal action is an "undertaking" and whether it has the potential to cause effects on historic properties. If so, then the federal agency official determines the appropriate SHPO to be involved in the consultation process. If the proposed undertaking would "occur on or affect historic properties on any tribal lands," then the federal agency official must determine whether the tribe has assumed the roles of the SHPO for tribal lands. If so, the THPO takes the place of the SHPO. This principle is reflected throughout the revised regulations through the use of the term "SHPO/THPO" rather than simply "SHPO." Even where a tribe has not assumed the role of the SHPO, this section provides that the tribe has a right to participate in consultation "in addition to and on the same basis as consultation with the SHPO." With respect to undertakings that affect historic properties not on tribal lands, this section of the regulations provides that the federal agency official:

> "[S]hall make a reasonable and good faith effort to identify any Indian tribes or Native Hawaiian organizations that might attach religious and cultural significance to historic properties in the area of potential effects and invites them to be consulting parties. Such Indian tribe or Native Hawaiian organization that requests in writing to be a consulting party shall be one."

Step 2 – Identification of Historic Properties. This step consists of four parts: (a) determine the scope of identification efforts; (b) identify historic properties; (c) evaluate historic significance; and (d) document the results of identification and evaluation.

(a) *Scope of Identification Effort.* The federal agency begins this step by consulting with the SHPO/THPO to determine the area of potential effects, review the existing information about historic properties in the area, and seek information from consulting parties and others. This section also includes a mandate to gather information from any Indian tribe or Native Hawaiian organization (NHO) regarding historic properties that may hold religious and cultural significance for them, recognizing that the tribe or NHO may be reluctant to divulge specific information.

(b) *Identify Historic Properties.* The federal agency does this in consultation with the SHPO/THPO and with any tribe or NHO that might attach religious and cultural significance to properties in the area of potential effects. The agency's mandate is to "take the steps necessary to identify historic properties," which may include "background research, oral history interviews, sample filed investigation, and field survey." The agency official must make a "reasonable and good faith effort." Identification of historic properties can require a substantial commitment of resources, and the regulations allow this to be done in a phased process in certain situations: where alternatives being considered include corridors and large land areas; where a Memorandum of Agreement or Programmatic Agreement authorizes phased identification; and where documents prepared for compliance with the National Environmental Policy Act (NEPA) so provide.

   (c) *Evaluate Historic Significance.* This means applying the National Register Criteria, 36 C.F.R. pt. 63, and determining whether any of the properties in the area of potential effects is eligible for the National Register. As with identification, the federal agency does this in consultation with the SHPO/THPO and with any tribe or NHO that might attach religious and cultural significance to properties in the area of potential effects. If the agency official and the SHPO/THPO agree, either that a property is eligible or that it is not, that generally settles that issue. If, however, the Advisory Council or the Secretary of the Interior (acting through NPS) requests a formal determination of eligibility by NPS, then the agency official must request a formal determination. A tribe or NHO that attaches religious and cultural significance to a historic property located off tribal lands may ask the Council to request a formal determination.

   (d) *Results of Identification and Evaluation.* If the agency official determines that there are no historic properties, or that there are historic properties but they will not be affected, the agency official provides documentation to the SHPO/THPO and notice to other consulting parties. If the SHPO/THPO does not object within thirty days, and neither does the Council, the federal agency official's section 106 responsibilities are fulfilled. If the agency official determines that the undertaking will affect historic properties, or either the SHPO/THPO or Council objects to a no effect finding, the consultation process moves on to the next step.

   Step 3 –Assessment of Adverse Effects. This section sets out criteria for determining whether effects on historic properties would be adverse, along with examples, and directs the federal agency official to apply these criteria in consultation with the SHPO/THPO and any tribe or NHO that attaches religious and cultural significance to identified historic properties. If the agency official, in consultation with the SHPO/THPO, proposes a finding of no adverse effect, notice and documentation must be provided to all the consulting parties. If within thirty days the SHPO/THPO or any consulting party expresses disagreement with the finding, the agency official must either consult with the party to resolve the disagreement or request the Advisory Council to review the finding. The agency official is encouraged to seek concurrence in a no adverse effect finding from any tribe or NHO that has let the agency official know that it attaches religious and cultural significance to identified historic properties, whether or not such a tribe or NHO is a consulting party. If such a tribe or NHO objects to the finding, it can request the Council to review the finding. If the Council does review the finding and determines that the effect would be adverse, the agency is bound by the Council's determination. If this step results in a finding of no adverse effect, that concludes the Section 106 process. If this step results in an adverse effect finding, however, the process moves to the next step.

   Step 4 –Resolution of Adverse Effects. In this step, the federal agency official, in consultation with the SHPO/THPO and other consulting parties, including tribes and NHOs, develops and evaluates alternative to avoid, minimize or mitigate adverse effects. The Advisory Council does not normally participate in this step, but it may choose to participate on its own initiative or at the request of the SHPO/THPO, a tribe or NHO, or another consulting party. Appendix A to the revised regulations specifies the criteria the Council will use in deciding whether to become involved in individual Section 106 cases. Criterion (4) provides that the Council is likely to enter the process when an undertaking presents issues of concern to Indian tribes or NHOs.

The objective of this step is to reach agreement on acceptable ways to avoid, minimize or mitigate adverse effects. Although all of the consulting parties participate in this step, in most cases only the federal agency official and the SHPO (or THPO for tribal lands) must actually reach agreement, as expressed in a Memorandum of Agreement. If the Council participates, then it must also by a signatory to the MOA. For historic properties off tribal lands, the agency official "may" invite a concerned tribe to be a signatory, and the signatories "should" invite any party that assumes responsibility under an MOA to become a signatory. The refusal of an invited party to sign, however, does not invalidate the MOA. In the event that consultation does not lead to an agreement on ways to avoid, minimize or mitigate adverse effects, the agency official, SHPO/THPO or the Council may decide that further consultation will not be productive. In such a case, the process will move on to a fifth step.

Step 5 – Failure to Resolve Adverse Effects. The outcome of this step may turn on which party terminates consultation. If the federal agency official terminates consultation, then the agency must request the Advisory Council to comment on the undertaking. The request must be made by "the head of the agency or an Assistant Secretary or other officer with major department-wide or agency-wide responsibilities." If the SHPO terminates consultation, the agency official and the Council may continue consultation and execute an MOA without the SHPO's involvement. If the THPO terminates consultation, the agency official and the Council cannot execute an MOA, and the Council provides comments on the undertaking.

In any case in which the process does not conclude in an MOA, Section 110(l) of the Act, 16 U.S.C. § 470h-2(l), provides that a decision to proceed with the undertaking must be made by the head of the agency, and that this decision-making responsibility cannot be delegated. Section 800.7(c)(4) of the regulations incorporates this statutory requirement. The agency head's decision must include a summary of the decision that contains the rationale for the decision and evidence of consideration of the Council's comments.

Native American Graves Protection and Repatriation Act
25 U.S.C. §§ 3001-3013, 18 U.S.C. § 1170

The Native American Graves Protection and Repatriation Act (NAGPRA) establishes rights of ownership or control over Native American human remains and certain kinds of "cultural items" (funerary objects, sacred objects, and objects of cultural patrimony) in two kinds of situations:

Repatriation These provisions of NAGPRA apply to human remains and cultural items that are under the custody of federal agencies or "museums" that receive federal funds (including state and local government agencies); and

Graves protection   These provisions of NAGPRA apply to human remains and cultural items that are embedded in the ground on federal lands or "tribal lands" (a term that includes all lands within the exterior boundaries of any Indian reservation, all dependent Indian communities, and certain lands administered for the benefit of Native Hawaiians).

Both the repatriation provisions of NAGPRA and the graves protection provisions establish requirements for consultation with tribes. These consultation requirements are implemented through regulations issued by the Secretary of the Interior (acting through the National Park Service). 43 C.F.R. part 10. In the context of the review of proposed federal actions that are likely to have effects on the environment, the graves protection provisions of NAGPRA may apply, if federal lands or tribal lands would be affected by the proposed federal action. The consultation requirements of NAGPRA's graves protection provisions are summarized below. These provisions may arise in either of two contexts: intentional excavations or inadvertent discoveries.

1.   *Intentional Excavations.*   NAGPRA uses the issuance of a permit under the Archaeological Resources Protection Act (ARPA) as a mechanism to protect Native American graves and imbedded cultural items. Excavation or removal form federal lands or tribal lands is prohibited unless an ARPA permit has been issued. 25 U.S.C. § 3002(c).

(a)   *Federal Lands.*   Notice and consultation with the culturally affiliated tribe (or NHO) is required prior to issuance of a permit. While consent is not a requirement for the issuance of a permit, the culturally affiliated tribe (or NHO) has the right to determine the ultimate disposition of any excavated human remains or cultural items. *See* 43 C.F.R. §§ 10.3, 10.5.

(b)   *Tribal Lands.*   Consent of the tribe (or NHO) is required. BIA is the permitting authority, including permits for lands within reservation boundaries other than trust or restricted Indian lands. *Id.* § 10.3(b)(1).

2.   *Discovery Situations.*   If Native American human remains or cultural items are discovered on federal lands or tribal lands, NAGPRA requires that the activity that led to such discovery cease. Any person making such a discovery must provide notice to the responsible federal agency official, for discoveries on federal lands, and the responsible tribal official for discoveries on tribal lands. 25 U.S.C. § 3002(d); 43 C.F.R. § 10.4. For discoveries on federal lands, the federal official then must provide notice to the appropriate tribe or NHO. The activity that led to the discovery may be resumed thirty days after certification that notice has been received. If resumption of the activity would require excavation or removal of human remains or cultural items, an ARPA permit is required. 43 C.F.R. § 10.4(d)(v), (e)(iii).

In the event that Native American human remains or cultural items are removed from federal lands or tribal lands, section three of NAGPRA, 25 U.S.C. § 3002, sets out the rules for determining who has rights of ownership or control over the human remains or cultural items. For human remains and associated funerary objects, lineal descendants have the highest priority. If lineal descendants cannot be ascertained, and for unassociated funerary objects, sacred objects and objects of cultural patrimony, if the items were discovered on tribal lands, the tribe on whose lands they were discovered has the right of ownership or control. If such items were found on federal lands, the tribe with the closest cultural affiliation has the right of ownership and control. If the federal lands where the discovery was made have been determined by the Indian Claims Commission or Court of Claims to be the aboriginal lands of a tribe, that tribe has a presumptive right of ownership or control unless another tribe makes a stronger showing of cultural affiliation. (The map of Indian land areas judicially established, prepared by the Indian Claims Commission in 1977, is available at: <www.wes.army.mil/el/ccspt/natamap/usa_pq.html>.) The procedure for determining rights of custody to such items is governed by the NAGPRA regulations. 43 C.F.R. § 10.6.

Federal Power Act
16 U.S.C. §§ 791-828(c)

The Federal Power Act (FPA) requires the Federal Energy Regulatory Commission (FERC or the Commission) to issue a license to all new hydropower projects built by anyone other than the federal government. These licenses are for a fixed period of time, and once the time limit has expired, a new license must be issued. The relicensing process allows state and federal agencies, conservation groups, Indian tribes, and the general public to comment on the proposed license.

1. *Consultation Requirements for Relicensing of Licensed Projects.* Before it files any application for a new license, non-power license, an exemption from licensing, or surrender of a project, a potential applicant must consult with various federal or state agencies and any Indian tribe that may be affected by the project. There are three stages of consultation the potential applicant must go through, with varying degrees of consultation with affected tribes.

(a) *First Stage of Consultation.* The potential applicant must provide agencies and Indian tribes with detailed information including maps, general engineering design, summary of operational mode, identification of the affected environment and mitigation plans, water regime information, and proposed studies. 18 C.F.R. § 16.8(b)(1)(i-vii). Within thirty to sixty days from the time the information has been sent, the potential applicant will hold a joint meeting, along with an opportunity for a site visit with all pertinent agencies and tribes. The issues to be discussed and the time and place of the meeting will be given to each agency, tribe, and the Commission at least fifteen days in advance. *Id.* § 16.8(b)(2)(i-ii).

No later than sixty days after the joint meeting each Indian tribe must provide the potential applicant with written comments identifying necessary studies to be performed or information to be provided by the potential applicant. The studies, known as additional information requests (AIRs), must include: (1) a study description; (2) the study objectives; (3) an explanation of the resource issues and its goals and objectives for those resources; (4) an explanation of why the study methodology recommended is more appropriate than that currently being used; (5) a statement of whether the methodology is generally accepted in the scientific community; and (6) an explanation of how the study will be useful to the tribe in furthering its goals and objectives. *Id.* § 16.8(b)(4)(i-vi).

If the tribe and potential applicant disagree as to any matter arising during the first stage of consultation, or to the need to conduct a study, the dispute may be referred in writing to the Director of the Office of Hydropower Licensing (the Director) for resolution. *Id.* § 16.8(b)(5)(i). The party entering the dispute must serve a copy of the request for resolution to the disagreeing party at the time the dispute is submitted to the Director. The disagreeing party may submit a written response to the Director within fifteen days of receiving the copy of the request for resolution. *Id.* § 16.8(b)(5)(ii). The request for resolution and responses must be filed with the Secretary of the Commission with an indication that they are for the attention of the Director of the Office of Hydropower Licensing. The Director will resolve disputes by letter to the potential applicant and disagreeing tribe. The first stage of consultation ends when all participating agencies and tribes provide the written comments or sixty days after the joint meeting, whichever occurs first. *Id.* § 16.8(b)(6).

      (b)   *Second Stage of Consultation.* A potential applicant must complete all reasonable and necessary studies and obtain all reasonable and necessary information requested by tribes in the first stage of consultation prior to filing the application if the results: would influence the financial or technical feasibility of the project; are needed to determine the design or location of project features, alternatives to the project, impact of the project on natural or cultural resources, mitigation or enhancement measures, or to minimize impact on significant resources. *Id.* § 16.8(c)(1)(i)(A)-(B).

A potential applicant must complete all reasonable and necessary studies and obtain all reasonable and necessary information requested by tribes in the first stage of consultation after the filing the application but before the issuance of the license provided it has produced the appropriate information described in 18 C.F.R. § 16.8(b)(1) no later than four years prior to the expiration of the existing license and the results are those described in 18 C.F.R. § 16.8(c)(1)(i)(A or B) and would take longer to conduct and evaluate than the time between the consultation and new license application filing date. *Id.* § 16.8(c)(1)(ii)

A potential applicant must complete all reasonable and necessary studies and obtain all reasonable and necessary information requested by tribes in the first stage of consultation after a new license is issued if the studies can be conducted and the information obtained only after construction or operation of the proposed facilities would determine the success of protection, mitigation, enhancement measures, or would be used to refine project operation or modify project facilities. *Id.* § 16.8(c)(1)(iii).

If, after the first stage of consultation is over, the tribe requests an AIR not previously identified, the potential applicant will promptly initiate the study or gather the information unless the Director determines the study is unreasonable or unnecessary or that the methodology used is not a generally accepted practice. *Id.* § 16.8(c)(2).

The potential applicant shall provide each resource agency and Indian tribe with a copy of its draft application. The draft application shall indicate the type of application to be filed with the Commission and respond to any comments and recommendations made by the tribe through AIRs including a discussion of the results and any proposed protection, mitigation, or enhancement measures for resources of interest to the tribe and which were identified in the first stage of consultation. The potential applicant should also include a written request for review and comment.

Id. § 16.8(c)(4).

An Indian tribe will have ninety days from the date of the potential applicant's letter to provide written comments. If the written comments indicate that a tribe has a substantive disagreement with a potential applicant's conclusions regarding resource impacts or proposed protection, mitigation, or enhancement measures the potential applicant should hold at least one joint meeting with the disagreeing tribe and other agencies with similar or related areas of interest, expertise, or responsibility. The joint meeting should take place no later than sixty days from the date of the tribe's written comments. The joint meeting should attempt to reach agreement on the potential applicant's plan for environmental protection, mitigation, or enhancement measures. The potential applicant shall consult with the disagreeing tribe and other agencies with similar or related areas of interest, expertise, or responsibility on the scheduling of the joint meeting. The potential applicant shall also provide both the tribe, interested agencies, and the Commission written notice of the time and place of each meeting and a written agenda of the issues to be discussed at least fifteen days in advance. *Id.* § 16.8(c)(5)-(6)(ii).

The potential applicant and disagreeing tribes may conclude the joint meeting with a document stating any agreement regarding environmental protection, mitigation, or enhancement measures and any issues left unresolved. *Id.* § 16.8(c)(7). In the potential applicant's application, all disagreements with resource agencies or Indian tribes must be described, including an explanation of the basis for the disagreement and any document developed during the joint meeting. *Id.* § 16.8(c)(8).

The second stage of consultation ends ninety days after the potential applicant submits a copy of its draft application to resource agencies and Indian tribes when no substantive disagreements have been registered. If a resource agency or tribe indicates a disagreement with the draft application, the second stage of consultation ends at the conclusion of the last joint meeting. *Id.* § 16.8(c)(10)(i-ii).

(c) ***Third Stage of Consultation.*** The third stage of consultation begins with the filing of an application for a new license, non-power license, exemption from licensing, or surrender of license accompanied by a letter certifying that copies of the application are being mailed to the resource agencies, Indian tribes, and other government officers. The potential applicant must provide copies of its application for a license, any deficiency correction, revision supplement, response to AIRs, or amendments to the application, and any written correspondence from the Commission requesting correction of deficiencies or submittal of additional information. *Id.* § 16.8(d)(2)(i-iii).

2. ***Compliance with Consultation Requirements.*** If a tribe waives in writing compliance with any requirement of 18 C.F.R. § 16.8, a potential applicant is not required to comply with requirements in regard to the tribe. *Id.* § 16.8(e)(1). If a tribe fails to timely comply with a provision, the potential applicant may proceed to the next sequential requirement without waiting for the tribe to comply. *Id.* § 16.8(e)(2). However, a tribe's failure to comply with a provision regarding a requirement of 18 C.F.R. § 16.8 does not preclude its participation in subsequent stages of the consultation process. *Id.* § 16.8(e)(3).

3. *Application Documentation.* An application for a license requires the potential applicant to include documentation of consultation and any disagreements with resource agencies or tribes. These documents must be included in Exhibit E of the application. Exhibit E must include: (1) any tribe's letters containing comments, recommendations, and proposed terms and conditions; (2) letters from the public containing comments and recommendations; (3) notice of any remaining disagreement with a tribe on the need for a study or information on any environmental protection, mitigation, or enhancement measure and the applicant's reason for disagreement with the tribe; (4) evidence of any consultation requirement waivers by the tribe; (5) evidence of all attempts to consult with the tribe, including copies of documents showing the attempts and the conclusion of the second stage of consultation; (6) an explanation of how and why the project would, would not, or should not comply with a plan as defined in section 2.19; (7) a copy of water quality certification, copy of request for certification, evidence of waiver of water quality certification; and (8) a statement showing how the applicant's proposal addresses issues raised by the public. *Id.* § 16.8(f)(1-8).

4. *Other Meetings.* Prior to holding a meeting with a resource agency or tribe the potential applicant must provide the Commission and any resource agency or tribe (with similar interests, expertise, or responsibility to the agency or tribe with which the potential applicant is meeting) with written notice of the time and place of each meeting and a written agenda of the issues to be discussed at least fifteen days in advance. *Id.* 16.8(h).

5. *Public Participation.* At least fourteen days in advance of the joint meeting, held in the first stage of consultation, the potential applicant must publish at least one notice of the purpose, location, and timing of the joint meeting in a daily or weekly newspaper published in the county or counties in which the existing project or any part thereof or the lands affected thereby are situated. The notice must include a written agenda of the issues to be discussed at the joint meeting. *Id.* § 16.8(i)(1). A potential applicant should make available to the public for reading and reproduction all information detailed in 18 C.F.R. § 16.8(b)(1). The information should be available from fourteen days in advance of the joint meeting until the date of the joint meeting. *Id.* § 16.8(i)(2)(i)

Nuclear Waste Policy Act of 1982
42 U.S.C. §§ 10101-10270 (1994)

Congress passed the Nuclear Waste Policy Act (NWPA) to establish federal policy for the responsible disposal of high-level radioactive waste and spent nuclear fuel. The Act establishes rules for the siting, construction, and operation of waste repositories "that will provide a reasonable assurance that the public and the environment will be adequately protected from the hazards posed by high-level radioactive waste." 42 U.S.C. § 10131(b). In order to fulfill this purpose, the Act requires the Department of Energy, the Nuclear Regulatory Commission, and any other agency involved in the siting, construction, or regulation of nuclear waste storage facilities to actively include affected tribes in the decision making process. 42 U.S.C. § 10121. The Act requires the Secretary to notify the governing body of any Indian tribe whenever a nuclear waste repository is proposed to be located on tribal lands. 42 U.S.C. § 10121(a). Following receipt of such notification, "affected tribes" are entitled to certain rights of participation and consultation. 42 U.S.C. § 10121(b). The Act defines "affected tribes" as not only those within whose reservations a facility is proposed to be located, but also those whose "federally defined usage rights" may be, in the opinion of the

Secretary, substantially and adversely affected by the proposed facility.

1. **_Right to Information._** Agencies involved in the proposed project must provide to the affected tribes, timely and complete information regrading the plans for siting, developing, constructing, operating, and decommissioning the proposed facility. 42 U.S.C. § 10137(a)(1). In addition, tribes may request information from the Secretary, who must respond with a written response within thirty days. 42 U.S.C. § 10137(a)(2). This response should include either the information requested or the reasons why the information cannot be so provided. _Id._ If the Secretary fails to respond within thirty days, the tribe can file a formal objection to the President. _Id._ If the President or Secretary fails to respond within thirty days of the receipt of the objection, the Secretary is required suspend all activities in developing the repository and shall not renew activities until he proper response to the tribe's request is made. _Id._

2. **_Right to Consultation and Cooperation._** Whenever any study is conducted to determine the suitability of an area for a repository, the Secretary shall consult and cooperate with and affected Indian tribe regarding the health, safety, environmental, and economic impacts of the propped facility. 42 U.S.C. § 10137(b). In developing plans for a nuclear-waste facility, the Secretary must take into account the concerns of the tribe "to the maximum extent feasible..." _Id.._ Federal regulations also require consultation with the affected tribes to determine whether the social and economic impacts of a proposed facility can be offset by reasonable mitigation and compensation. 10 C.F.R. § 960.5-2-6.

3. **_Written Agreement._** Within sixty days after the tribe is notified of the proposed project, the Secretary shall seek to enter into a binding written agreement with the tribes that sets forth the procedures for consultation and cooperation with the tribe. 42 U.S.C. § 10137(c). The agreement should be completed within six months and should describe, among other things, how to study the safety, economic, social and environmental impacts of the proposed facility, how the Secretary will respond to comments and recommendations from the tribal government, how to share information and resources, and how objections should be resolved. _Id._ The document, which cannot affect the ultimate authority of the Commission, must also establish procedures to periodic review and modification of the agreement. _Id._

4. **_Right to On-site Representative and Financial Assistance._** To help empower the tribe to actively participate in the siting decision, the Act offers affected tribes the opportunity and funding to appoint a representative to conduct on-site oversight activities. 42 U.S.C. § 10137(d). In addition, the Act authorizes the Secretary to provide grants to help affected tribes study the impacts of the project, develop recommendations, engage in monitoring and testing, and to educate tribal members regarding the siting proposal. 42 U.S.C. § 10138(b). Within six months after construction of a facility is authorized, the Secretary shall also make available additional funds to help tribes mitigate the impacts of the project. To receive any financial assistance under the Act, an affected tribe must submit a detailed report to the Secretary describing any economic, social, health, or environmental impacts that are likely to result from the development of the repository facility. _Id._ The details of any payments made to the tribes pursuant to the Act should be set forth in the written consultation agreement. _Id._

5. **_Right to Petition Congress._** If the consultation process does not result in a favorable

agreement, the tribe may submit a formal petition to Congress expressing the tribe's disapproval of the proposed project. 42 U.S.C. § 10138. Once Congress has received the petition objecting to the siting decision, the designation of the proposed site will not be effective, unless both houses pass a resolution within ninety days specifically approving the proposed plan. 42 U.S.C. § 1034(b)-(c).

Intermodal Surface Transportation Efficiency Act of 1991
23 U.S.C. §§ 102-189 (1999 Supp.)

The Intermodal Surface Transportation Efficiency Act (ISTEA) is a highway appropriations statute that replaced the recently expired Federal Aid Highway Act that provided state's with funding to construct and maintain the U.S. interstate system. Under the new Act, the Secretary of Transportation may make grants to states with federally approved highway programs. 23 U.S.C. § 133(b). The Secretary may withhold highway funding, however, if a state fails to substantially comply with the provisions of the Act. 23 U.S.C. § 133(e)(1). To withhold funding, the Secretary must first give the state notice that it is out of compliance, and allow the state sixty days to take corrective action.

ISTEA requires states to develop state-wide long-range transportation plans and all federally funded transportation projects in the state must be consistent with the plan. 23 U.S.C. § 135. In developing the plans that include Indian country, states must consult with affected tribal governments and specifically address their concerns. 23 U.S.C. § 135(d)(2), (f)(1)(iii). While the Act does not speak directly to the duration of the consultation requirement, the fact that transportation-improvement plans are subject to the Secretary's biennial review suggests that the Act requires ongoing consultation with tribal officials. 23 U.S.C. § 135(f)(4).

Alaska National Interest Lands Conservation Act
16 U.S.C. §§ 3102-3203 (1994 & Supp. 2000)

As amended, the Alaska National Interest Lands Conservation Act (ANILCA) is designed "to protect and provide the opportunity for continued subsistence uses on the public lands by native and non-native rural residents." 16 U.S.C. § 3111(4). In addition, the Act "enable[s] rural residents who have personal knowledge of local conditions and requirements to have a meaningful role in the management of fish and wildlife..." *Id.* § 3111(5). To accomplish these goals, the statute allows the Department of the Interior to enter into cooperative agreements with tribal organizations to effectuate the purposes and policies of the Act. *Id.* § 3119. The Secretary is also required to undertake studies on subsistence uses, and in doing so, must seek data from and consult with local residents. *Id.* § 3122.

ANILCA requires the Secretary to provide public participation opportunities to rural communities whenever an agency action would significantly restrict subsistence uses in a particular area. 16 U.S.C. § 3120(a). Specifically, no such action can take place unless the Secretary of the Interior gives prior notice to local communities and advisory committees established pursuant to 16 U.S.C. section 3115. Id. § 3120(a)(1). In addition, the Secretary is must hold hearings in the area affected by the agency action. *Id.* § 3120(2). It should be noted, however, that the Ninth Circuit has held that ANILCA is not "Indian legislation," and therefore does not give Alaska Native communities the benefit of the traditional rule that requires courts to interpret ambiguous statutes in favor of the tribes. *See* Hoonah Indian Assoc. v. Morrison, 170 F.3d 1223, 1228-29 (9th Cir. 1999).

NOTE: This Addendum is not intended to represent a complete listing of all federal laws and regulations that require or authorize consultation with tribes.

VARIOUS AGENCY CONSULTATION PROTOCOLS AND GUIDELINES

In response to President Clinton's April 29, 1994 Memorandum on Government-to Government Relationships, many agency's have developed programs and protocols to guide government officials in the consultation process. This addendum will provide brief descriptions of intra-agency documents, memorandum, and policies that specifically address consultation with tribal governments. In addition, many of these sources are readily available on-line, and this addendum will provide web addresses whenever applicable. IPS requests input from agencies and all parties and is open to suggestions on additional documents to be referenced in this addendum.

A.   Guidelines Developed in Coordination withe Tribal Governments

U.S. EPA REGION 10, TRIBAL CONSULTATION FRAMEWORK (2000) (draft version).

In this draft document, EPA Region Ten (Region) outlines its policies for encouraging regular participation by Indian tribes in Agency decisions affecting tribal members and resources. The document provides guiding principles for a government-to-government relationship and defines consultation as "two-way communication that works toward a consensus reflecting the concerns of the affected federally recognized tribe(s)."

On specific matters affecting tribes, the Region is to contact the tribes as early as practicable. The document also explains that it will not challenge the tribe's legal right to consultation whenever a specific Indian trust resource is involved and will try to hold meetings in Indian country to the extent resources allow. The document recognizes that consultation is separate from public participation. Consequently, the Region will conduct a separate public participation process for all interested stakeholders.

The Region has also provided for a method of issue resolution that first tries to resolves disputes between the Agency and a tribe informally, at the staff level. If the dispute is not resolved, supervisors will attempt to negotiate a workable solution. In an agreement is still not reached, the Agency and tribe will issue progressively higher levels of management until consensus is reached. The EPA Regional administrator is the final arbitrator of the dispute who will make his or her decision after consultation with the elected tribal leader(s).

B.   Protocols Developed Independently by Agencies

On November 8, 1993, the Interior Secretary Bruce Babbitt issued Secretarial Order No. 3175 which required all departments to consult with tribal governments whenever tribal resources could be potentially affected by a proposed agency action. In addition the departments were to publish directives or policies to ensure that staff were familiar with the Secretaries mandate and that the departments were in compliance with the order. The Order was latter incorporated into the Agencies Departmental Manual. *See* DEPARTMENT OF THE INTERIOR, DEPARTMENTAL MANUAL pt. 512, ch. 2. (1995). Under the Agency's policy, consultation's by departments must be respectful of tribal sovereignty and the Agency must be prepared to explain how its decision is consistent with the trust doctrine. *See id.* ch. 2.4.

1.   U.S. FISH AND WILDLIFE SERVICE, NATIVE AMERICAN POLICY (1994).

In its formal policies, the Fish and Wildlife Service (USFWS) recognizes that "there is a distinctive political relationship between the United States and Native American governments" and "supports the authority of Native American governments to manage, co-manage, or cooperatively manage fish and wildlife resources, and to protect their Federally recognized authorities." U.S. FISH AND WILDLIFE SERVICE, NATIVE AMERICAN POLICY 3, 4 (1994). To effectuate to this policy, USFWS will consult with tribal governments to the extent allowed by law. *See id.* at 5. For activities affecting tribal fish and wildlife resources on non-reservation lands, USFWS will still give tribes opportunities to participate in the Agency's decision-making process. *See id.* at 4.

The policy explains how USFWS will also coordinate enforcement of federal wildlife laws with the tribe, including in areas bordering Indian country. *See id.* at 6. In addition, USFWS will develop partnership agreements with tribes to facilitate the exchange of technical expertise regarding wildlife conservation and recovery. *See id.* The policy also directs the Service to provide training and other professional development opportunities to tribal members to assist tribes in developing cooperative wildlife management programs. *See id.* at 7.

2.   BUREAU OF LAND MANAGEMENT, NO. H-8160-1, GENERAL PROCEDURAL GUIDANCE FOR NATIVE AMERICAN CONSULTATION (1994), *available at* **http://lm0005.blm.gov/nhp/efoia/wo/handbook/h8160-1.html.**

In 1994, the Bureau of Land Management (BLM) published a handbook on consultation procedures to help assure "that tribal governments, Native American communities, and individuals whose interests might be affected have a sufficient opportunity for productive participation in BLM planning and resource management decision making." BUREAU OF LAND MANAGEMENT, NO. H-8160-1, GENERAL PROCEDURAL GUIDANCE FOR NATIVE AMERICAN CONSULTATION ch. I., pt. A. (1994). Although the handbook includes individuals in its definition of "consultation," it also recognizes that the "[s]overign status of Indian tribes and special provisions of law set Native Americans apart from all other U.S. populations and define a special level of Federal agency responsibilities." *Id.* ch. I., at pt. D. In light of these unique responsibilities, the Handbook sets forth a Consultation and Documentation Standard:

> Before making decisions or approving actions that could result in change in land use, physical changes to lands, or resources, changes in access, or alienation of lands, BLM managers must determine whether Native American interests would be affected, observe pertinent consultation requirements, and document how this was done. In the face of legal challenge, the consultation record will be the BLM's basis for demonstrating that the responsible manager has made a reasonable and good faith effort to obtain and consider appropriate Native American input in decision making. *Id.* ch. 1, at pt. B.

Under the Agency's policy as described in the Handbook, consultation is designed to not only identify tribal interests and concerns, but also to examine the tribes suggestions on how to effectively address the concerns. *See id.* ch. II, at pt. E. "Consultation is incomplete, and largely pointless, unless its is directed toward the identification of mutually acceptable solutions." *Id.* When tribal cultural and religious natural resources are involved, these solutions may require something different from the traditional analysis of mitigation options found in statutes such as NEPA and NHPA. *See id.* pt. D.

The Handbook describes the step-by-step process of the BLM should follow in carrying out consultation. *See generally id.* ch. III (setting forth guidance to help "establish ongoing, credible consultation relationships"). For example, the Handbook describes how staff must identify the appropriate parties to consult, including officials form recognized tribes, representatives of non-recognized Indian communities, traditional religious and cultural leaders, and lineal descendants of deceased Native Americans whose remains are in federal possession or control. *See id* pt. B. In deciding whether the level consultation is sufficient, Agency staff must examine on a case-by-case basis: (1) the potential for harm caused by the proposed action; (2) alternatives which would reduce the harm and disruption; (3) whether all appropriate tribal groups have been consulted; (4) the nature of the issues raised; (5) the intensity of the concern expressed; (6) the legal requirements of treaties; (7) the productivity of the consultation; and (7) the need for further consultation. *Id.* pt. E.

3. NATIONAL PARK SERVICE, PROTECTION OF INDIAN TRUST RESOURCES (1995).

Section four of this document explains that NPS will consult with tribal governments on matters of mutual interest and concern. Consultation procedures to provide direct participation should be developed with tribal governments and privacy and confidentiality shall be respected "to the extent allowed by law." In addition, the document calls on the agency to provide staff training to improve its employees' understanding of the government-to-government relationship, trust responsibilities, and tribal culture and history.

CONSULTATION GUIDING PRINCIPLES AND CRITICAL ELEMENTS

The following outline of guiding principles and critical elements for consultation with Indian tribes is based on the text set forth in Chapter 3 of this Guide, titled "Methods for Effective Consultation." The outline highlights key points found in that Chapter's more detailed discussion.

GUIDING PRINCIPLES

A.   Know the Tribes

Federal agencies should know of: (1) all tribes within their jurisdiction including without limitation those tribes with jurisdiction over tribal land, who claim a historical, cultural, religious, customary, cultural, or aboriginal relationship with land within the agency's jurisdiction; (2) all tribal organizations within the agency's jurisdiction; (3) all tribes who may attach religious and cultural importance to historic places that may be affected by the agency's actions.

B.   Build Ongoing Consultative Relationships with Tribes

Conduct consultation within the framework of an ongoing government-to-government relationship. Ongoing relationships will help tribes and agencies best allocate their resources for purposes of consultation.

C.   Institutionalize Consultation and Collaboration Procedures

Work with tribes to develop formal consultation policies, and use a memorandum of agreement to document arrangements with a specific tribe. Publish agency consultation policies and procedures, and make them available to tribal governments and the affected public.

D.   Contact Tribes Early and Allow Sufficient Time to Consult

1.   Provide the tribe adequate time to formulate and to express its views, and consider tribal views before making decisions.
2.   Schedule consultation efforts to facilitate meaningful tribal consultation that is consistent with the federal trust responsibility owed to that tribe.
3.   Pursue consultation even if a tribe does not respond to initial requests to engage in consultation, and recognize that, based on historical dealings, some tribes may question whether their participation will be meaningful.

E.   Establish Ongoing Training Programs for all Staff on Consultation with Tribes

F.   Maintain Honesty and Integrity in the Consultation Process

G.   View Consultation as an Integral and Essential Element of the Government-to-Government Relationship with Tribes, and Not Simply As a Procedural Requirement

CRITICAL ELEMENTS OF CONSULTATION

A.   **Preparation for Consultation**

    1.   Be aware that tribes are culturally and administratively different from each other.
    2.   Allow ample time for the tribe to receive, process, and respond to requests for consultation.
    3.   Understand that some kinds of information are sensitive, particularly information regarding traditional religious practices.
    4.   Review any applicable agency consultation protocols and guidelines.

B.   **Participants in Consultation and Collaboration**

    1.   Identify tribal representative(s) who will serve as the contact(s) in the consultation process.
    2.   Determine if a tribe would prefer having federal agencies coordinate their consultative efforts to reduce the burden on tribal staff and other resources.
    3.   Consultation with inter-tribal organizations may be useful on issues of regional or national scope, however, such consultation is not a substitute for consultation with each tribe unless specifically authorized by the involved tribe or tribes.
    4.   At times, it may be advisable under certain federal laws (e.g. Native American Graves Protection and Repatriation Act and National Historic Preservation Act) to seek information from tribal members and traditional religious leaders in addition to those persons who have been formally designated by a tribe as contacts for consultation. The interests of traditional leaders and cultural authorities may not always coincide with those of tribal government.

C.   **Logistics and Mechanics**

    1.   Work within the government-to-government context, and strive to ensure interaction through officials of comparable governmental stature and authority.
    2.   Remember that tribal staff must have tribal government authorization to make policy decisions or to take tribal positions.
    3.   The goal of consultation should be direct, two-way dialogue.
    4.   Clearly and plainly describe the proposed action or policy to tribal representatives and community members.
    5.   Use informational meetings for larger audiences, and invite tribal contacts to attend or co-sponsor public meetings; however, do not substitute information meetings for separate agency meetings with tribal leadership, which is another essential element of consultation.
    6.   When appropriate to seek involvement from members of the affected public, consult with tribes about how to do effectively.
    7.   Work with tribal representatives to identify the ultimate goals of the consultation.

PUBLIC PARTICIPATION GUIDING PRINCIPLES AND CRITICAL ELEMENTS

The following set of guiding principles and critical elements for public participation in Indian county were developed using The Model Plan for Public Participation, a document created by the National Environmental Justice Advisory Committee. This Model Plan was redrafted for the purposes of making it more applicable to Indian country.

GUIDING PRINCIPLES

A.   Encourage Public Participation

Encourage public participation in all aspects of environmental decision making. Communities, including all types of stakeholders, should be seen as equal partners in dialogue on environmental and public health concerns in the community. In order to build successful partnerships, interactions must:

- Encourage active community participation
- Institutionalize public participation
- Recognize community knowledge
- Utilize cross-cultural formats and exchanges

B.   Maintain Honesty and Integrity

While working to involve the public in the decision making processes, it is very important that honesty and integrity be maintained. It is also important that the goals, expectations, and limitations be established at the very beginning.

CRITICAL ELEMENTS

A.   Preparation for Meetings

1.   Co-sponsor the Meeting

Developing co-sponsoring and co-planning relationships with community organizations is essential to successful community meetings. For this reason, governments should consider co-sponsoring the meeting with a community organization and should share all planning roles.

These roles include:
- Decision making
- Development of the agenda
- Establishment of clear goals
- Leadership
- Outreach

2.   Educate the Community

It is important to educate the community on the subject matter and the decision-making processes to allow for equal participation and provide a means to influence decision making.

3.   Provide a Facilitator

A facilitator can ensure the process is fair by objectively overseeing the deliberations and preventing any one group from being displaced in the process. The facilitator should be someone who is experienced and sensitive to community participation and trained in environmental issues.

B.   Participants

The following entities should be involved in environmental justice issues:
- Community and neighborhood groups
- Traditional leaders/elders
- Community service organizations (health, welfare, and others)
- Educational institutions and academia
- Environmental organizations
- Government agencies
- Industry and business
- Medical community
- Non-governmental organizations
- Religious communities

Identify key stakeholders, including:
- Educational institutions
- Affected communities
- Policy and decision makers (for example, representatives of agencies accountable for environmental and public health issues, regulatory and enforcement officials, and social agency staff).

C.   Logistics

1.   Where:
- The meetings should be accessible to all who wish to attend (public transportation, child care, and access for the disabled should be considered).
- The meeting must be held in an adequate facility (size and conditions must be considered).
- Technologies should be used to allow for more effective communication (teleconferences, adequate translation, equipment, and other factors).

2   When:
- The time of day and year of the meeting should accommodate the needs of affected communities (evening and weekend meetings accommodate working people, and careful scheduling can avoid conflicts with other community or cultural events).

3   How:
- An atmosphere of equal participation must be created (avoid using a "panel"

or "head table").

- An all day meeting may be necessary. The first part of the day should be reserved for community planning and education.
- The community and the government should share leadership and presentation assignments.

D. Mechanics

- Maintain clear goals by referring to the agenda; however, do not be bound by it.
- Incorporate cross-cultural exchanges in the presentation of information and the meeting agenda.
- Provide a professional facilitator who is sensitive to, and trained in, environmental justice issues.
- Provide a time line that describes how the meeting fits into the overall agenda of the issues at hand.
- Coordinate follow-up by developing an action plan and determining who is the contact person who will expedite the work products from the meeting.
- Distribute minutes and a list of action items to facilitate follow-up.

CORE VALUES: PRACTICE OF PUBLIC PARTICIPATION

1. People should have a say in decisions about actions which affect their lives.

2. Public participation includes the promise that the public's contribution will influence the decision.

3. The public participation process communicates the interests and meets the process needs of all participants.

4. The public participation process seeks out and facilitates the involvement of those potentially affected.

5. The public participation process involves participants in defining how they participate.

6. The public participation process communicates to participants how their input was, or was not, utilized.

7. The public participation process provides participants with the information they need to participate in a meaningful way.

Source: Interact: The Journal of Public Participation, Volume 2, Number 1, Spring 1996. Interact is published by the International Association of Public Participation Practitioners, a non profit corporation established in 1990 to serve practitioners throughout the world seeking practical experience designing and conducting public involvement programs.

GLOSSARY

Allotment: Surveyed reservation land distributed by the government to individual Indians under the provisions of the Dawes Allotment Act. Generally, 160 acres were allotted to heads of families; eighty acres to single persons; and forty acres to other family members.

Bureau of Indian Affairs (BIA): Agency within the U.S. Department of the Interior responsible for administering the U.S. government's relationships with Indian governments and for overseeing Congress's trust responsibility for Indian lands and existence.

Cession: The ceding or yielding of rights, property, or territory from one group or person to another.

Collaboration: To work together, in an intellectual effort.

Consultation: A collaborative process between government peers resulting in a consensus on how to proceed.

Consultation and Coordination with Indian Tribal Governments: This is the title of Executive Order 13084, signed by the President on May 14, 1998 that requires federal agencies to respect tribal self-government and sovereignty, tribal rights, and tribal responsibilities whenever they formulate policies that affect Indian tribal governments in a unique or significant way.

Council: A group elected or appointed as an advisory or legislative body; council members are usually equal in power and authority.

Culture: The ideas, customs, skills, arts, etc., of a given people in a given period.

Cultural Resources: Products of human activity or objects or places given significance by human action or belief; include places of historic significance, archeological sites and resources, graves and funery objects; also includes "traditional cultural properties" (see below).

Dawes Allotment Act: Also known as the General Allotment Act of 1887, this act required that communally held reservation lands be allotted to individual for ownership; reservation lands not so allotted were generally opened up by the federal government for settlement by non-Indians, often leading to troublesome 'checkerboard' jurisdictional issues.

Domestic Dependent Nation: Term used by Chief Justice John Marshall in 1831 to characterize the legal status of the Indian nations.

Environmental Justice: The fair treatment and meaningful involvement of all people regardless of race, color, national origin, or income with respect to the development, implementation and enforcement of environmental laws, regulations and policies. Fair treatment means that no group of people, including racial, ethnic or socioeconomic group should bear a disproportionate share of the negative environmental consequences resulting from industrial, municipal and commercial operations or the execution of federal, state, local and tribal programs and policies.

Environmental Protection Agency (EPA): EPA is a federal agency whose mission is "to protect human health and to safeguard the natural environment   air, water and land   upon which life depends. The Administrator of EPA reports directly to the President of the United States.

EPA Indian Programs: This program involves significant intra-Agency and multimedia activities designed to ensure protection of human health and the tribal environment, in a manner consistent with EPA's trust responsibility to federally-recognized tribes, the government-to-government relationship, and the conservation of cultural uses of natural resources. The underlying philosophy of this program is that tribal governments are the appropriate authorities to set goals for environmental and human health protection activities in Indian country.

EPA Policy on Environmental Programs on Indian Reservations: In 1984, EPA was the first federal agency outside the Department of the Interior to adopt a formal policy statement regarding Indian Tribes. This policy includes nine principles that guide EPA's relationship with Indian tribes and implementation of its programs on Indian reservations.

Ethnocentrism: The belief that one's own ethnic group and culture are superior to all others.

Federally Recognized Tribes: Tribes with whom the federal government maintains an official relationship, usually established by treaty, congressional legislation, or executive order. The Bureau of Indian Affairs maintains and regularly publishes the list of federally-recognized Indian tribes.

Government-to-Government Relationship: Relationship that exists between federally recognized tribes and the federal government. Implicit in the relationship is a recognition of tribal sovereignty as individual nations within the U.S. and the U.S. government's obligation to protect tribal lands. The relationship between tribal and state governments should also be characterized as government-to-government.

Indian Country: As defined by federal law, Indian country includes all land within the limits of any Indian reservation under the jurisdiction of the U.S. government, notwithstanding the issuance of any patent, and including rights-of-ways running through the reservation. In addition, Indian country also includes all dependent Indian communities as well as all Indian allotments to which Indian titles have not been extinguished.

Indian Sacred Sites: This is the title of Executive Order #13007 signed on May 24, 196 by the President that directs federal agencies that manage federal lands to accommodate access to and ceremonial use of Indian sacred sites and avoid adversely affecting the physical integrity of such sacred ties.

Jurisdiction: The legal authority a government has to govern its people and territory.

Litigation: Adversarial legal contest carried out through the judicial process.

Nation: A stable, historically developed community of people who share territory, economic life, distinctive culture, and language.

Native Americans: This term broadly describes the people considered indigenous to North America

52

who lived here prior to European colonization. The term includes "American Indians," "Indians," "Alaska Natives," "Eskimos," and "Aleuts," and "Native Hawai'ians."

Native Hawai'ians: These are people that can be described as Native American because they are indigenous to their areas. Native Hawai'ians, however, have a different relationship with the U.S. Government. As a group, they are not recognized as a legal, political entity or "government." Nevertheless, Native Hawai'ians are described as a discrete group in the Native American Programs Act of 1974 (NAPA).

Non-Intercourse Act: An act passed in 1790 that prohibited the sale of any Indian-owned land without the approval of the United States Congress.

Non-Recognized Tribe: Tribe with whom the federal government does not maintain a government-to-government relationship, and to which the federal government does not recognized a trust responsibility towards, resulting in a lack of provision of federal services based on their status as an Indian tribe or recognition of its land base or sovereignty.

Public Participation: When the public is informed of a proposed or actual action, and is provided meaningful opportunities to participate in the decision-making process.

Plenary Doctrine: Doctrine stating that the federal government has unlimited and exclusive authority and jurisdiction over Indian tribes. Because of this, states generally lack governmental authority over Indian tribes and tribal members within Indian country, unless Congress has expressly delegated authority to states.

Protectorate: Relationship between two sovereigns in which the weaker state places itself under the protection of the more powerful state.

Referendum: Process of submitting and issue to popular vote.

Relocation: Federal policy formulated in 1952. Indians were relocated from rural and reservation areas to urban areas for job training and employment.

Removal Act: Act passed by Congress in 1830 authorizing the president to negotiate with eastern tribes for their removal to lands west of the Mississippi River.

Reservation: Lands reserved by a tribe during treaty negotiations with the federal government for tribal use. Indian reservations are held in trust for the tribe by the federal government.

Reserved-Rights Doctrine: Doctrine enunciated by the courts that tribes retain all rights to their land, water, and resources unless they have expressly granted them to the federal government.

Self-Determination: Decision-making control over one's own affairs and the policies that affect one's life. This is also the name of the federal government's policy toward Indian nations, beginning in 1978.

Sovereign: Supreme in power or authority.

Sovereignty: The status, dominion, rule or power of a sovereign. Tribes have the power to make and enforce laws for their tribe and reservation, and to establish courts and other forums for resolution of disputes.

State-Recognized Tribes: Tribes that usually are not federally recognized but maintain a special relationship with their state government and whose lands and rights are recognized by the state.

Supplemental Environmental Projects (SEPS): SEPs are projects that are included in the settlement of a lawsuit involving a violation of an environmental statute administered by EPA. When such lawsuits are settled, a party may agree to pay for SEPs that include environmental restoration or enhancement.

Terminated Tribes: Tribes whose government-to-government and trust relationship with the federal government has been terminated. Most of the more than one hundred terminations occurred between 1954 and 1961.

Termination: Federal Indian policy formally adopted by the U.S. Congress in 1954 that sought to end the federal government's relationship with Indian tribes as prescribed under House Concurrent Resolution 108. President Richard Nixon formally ended this policy in 1971.

Tradition: Cultural beliefs and customs handed down from ancestors.

Traditional Cultural Properties (TCP's): Beliefs or practices of a people tied to land or water, in conjunction with religious beliefs and/or practices.

Treaty: Formal, legally binding contract between two sovereign nations; an agreement between two or more nations, relating to peace, alliance, trade, etc.

Tribe: A group of individuals bound together by ancestry, kinship, languages, culture, and political authority.

Trust: Property the title to which is legally held by one entity for the benefit of another.

Trust Doctrine: This is rooted in the treaties between Indian tribes and the U.S. government where Indian land was ceded to the government, under treaties, in exchange for protection of remaining tribal land and rights. Under this doctrine, the U.S. government holds title to Indian land in trust for the beneficial use of Indian tribes and their members. This includes other protection, including protection of the Indians' sovereign rights.

Trustee: Person to whom another's property, or the management of that property, is entrusted.

Trusteeship: Term referring to the federal government's legal obligation to protect tribal land, resources, and existence.

Unfounded Mandates Act: This act expressly authorized federal employees to talk to state employees and tribal employees without violating the Federal Advisory Committee act.

Village: Term used to denote a community of Alaskan natives.

Wardship: Refers to the federal government's responsibility as trustee over Indians as carried out primarily by the Bureau of Indian Affairs.

ADDENDUM F

MISSION STATEMENT
NATIONAL ENVIRONMENTAL JUSTICE ADVISORY COUNCIL
INDIGENOUS PEOPLES SUBCOMMITTEE

Preamble. In December 1995, two years after its creation, the U.S. Environmental Protection Agency's (EPA) National

Environmental Justice Advisory Council (NEJAC) created a subcommittee the Indigenous Peoples Subcommittee to advise the NEJAC on environmental justice issues facing Indigenous peoples. The NEJAC recognized that these unique issues require the specialized knowledge, experience, and expertise of the Subcommittee because of the government to government relationship between the sovereign Indian tribes and other governments, and because environmental injustices strike to the core of the cultural and political integrity of Indigenous communities.

Indigenous communities whether Hawaiian or Alaskan natives, federally recognized Indian tribes and their members, urban Indigenous peoples, non federally recognized Indigenous communities, or Indigenous communities across international boundaries all belong to a community of people whose ancestors inhabited this continent before European colonization. Since time immemorial, Indigenous peoples have lived a spiritual ethic that is founded upon a deeply held respect for the air, the water, the land, the plants, and the animals; an ethic that recognizes the essential link between the health of communities and the health of the ecosystems and cultures that sustain those communities.

Composition of the Subcommittee. Members of the Subcommittee are selected from the following groups: elders and spiritual leaders from Indigenous communities; individuals from Indigenous communities who have first hand knowledge of environmental justice issues facing Indigenous peoples; members of organizations that address environmental impacts on Indigenous communities; members of academia; representatives of federally recognized American Indian tribal governments that assert their sovereign powers to manage, protect, and restore tribal ecosystems; representatives of state and local governments that govern areas neighboring Indigenous communities; and representatives of industries that directly or indirectly impact indigenous communities. The Subcommittee also will work closely with the Designated Federal Official who is knowledgeable about federal environmental programs available to Indigenous peoples.

Mission. Together, members of the Subcommittee will draw upon their collective experiences, knowledge, and expertise to facilitate the NEJAC's formulation of recommendations and advice provided to EPA on environmental justice policy and direction as it affects Indigenous peoples. To achieve its mission, the Subcommittee will, at a minimum, perform the following functions:

Provide a forum for representatives of Indigenous communities, including grassroots organizations from within those communities, to bring their environmental justice concerns to the attention of the NEJAC and provide recommendations and advice to the NEJAC to address those concerns.

Provide recommendations and advice to the NEJAC on the development of EPA backed legislation, as well as Agency policy, guidance, and protocol, to help achieve environmental justice for Indigenous peoples.

Provide recommendations and advice to the NEJAC to ensure that environmental justice issues of concern to Indigenous peoples are addressed by EPA in a manner that fulfills the trust responsibility, respects tribal sovereignty and the government to government relationship, upholds treaties, and promotes tribal self determination.

Recognize that issues facing Indigenous peoples span the spectrum of issues addressed by other NEJAC subcommittees and interface with those subcommittees to ensure that all subcommittees address environmental justice issues of concern to Indigenous peoples in an informed manner.

www.ingramcontent.com/pod-product-compliance
Lightning Source LLC
Chambersburg PA
CBHW080906290526
45795CB00007BA/2435